Law

HUMAN RIGHTS

AUSTRALIA
LBC Information Services—Sydney

CANADA and USA
Carswell—Toronto

NEW ZEALAND
Brooker's—Auckland

SINGAPORE and MALAYSIA
Sweet & Maxwell Asia
Singapore and Kuala Lumpur

*Law*Basics

HUMAN RIGHTS

By

Dr Alastair N. Brown

Solicitor (Scotland; England & Wales)
Fellow of the Scottish Centre for International Law

EDINBURGH
W. GREEN/Sweet & Maxwell
2000

Published in 2000 by W. Green & Son Ltd
21 Alva Street
Edinburgh EH2 4PS

Printed in Great Britain by Athenaeum Press,
Gateshead, Tyne & Wear

No natural forests were destroyed to make this product;
Only farmed timber was used and replanted

A CIP catalogue record for this book is available from the British Library

ISBN 0 414 01398 0

© W. Green & Son Ltd 2000

For my parents, Ken and Evelyn Brown

CONTENTS

TABLE OF CASES

1. INTRODUCTION

This book is about human rights law as it applies in the national (or domestic) laws of the United Kingdom. That means that, although international human rights law is a very wide field indeed, almost everything written in this book is concerned with the European Convention on Human Rights and Fundamental Freedoms 1950 ("ECHR"). Other human rights treaties are only available for the use of national courts in the United Kingdom where the language of statute is ambiguous and one of the possible meanings is consistent with a treaty to which the United Kingdom is party while other possible meanings are not. In such a case, the treaty can be used as an aid to interpretation, on the presumption that Parliament intends to legislate in conformity with the United Kingdom's international obligations (*Salomon v. Commissioners of Customs and Excise* (1967); *T., Petitioner* (1997)). So far as ECHR is concerned, however, the effect of the Human Rights Act 1998 ("HRA") is to incorporate the Treaty into national law and require the courts to take it into account irrespective of any statutory ambiguity. In Chapter 2 we shall look at how it does that.

This Chapter introduces ECHR, the European Court of Human Rights ("the Court") and the general principles that apply to the application and interpretation of ECHR.

ECHR

The place of ECHR in international human rights law
ECHR represents only a very small part of international human rights law. As a whole, international human rights law consists of a wide range of texts, some binding and others merely recommendations. Some of those instruments are global, like the International Covenant on Civil and Political Rights 1976. Others (such as ECHR itself) are regional, in that they apply only in a particular part of the world. The American Convention on Human Rights 1969 and the African Charter on Human and Peoples Rights 1981 are other examples.

Some international human rights instruments are general in that they deal with a range of rights. Others, such as the European Convention for the Prevention of Torture and Inhuman or Degrading Treatment or Punishment 1987, deal with specific types of human rights violations. Others, such as the UN Convention on the Rights of the Child 1989, address the needs of particular sections of humanity.

It is common to treat international human rights law in three "generations":

(1) *Civil and Political Rights.* This includes ECHR and is, accordingly, the only "generation" dealt with in this book.

(2) *Economic, Social and Cultural Rights*. Examples include rights to an adequate standard of living, to food, clothing and housing and to take part in the cultural life of the community.

(3) *Collective or Peoples' Rights*. Examples include the right to development and the right of colonised peoples to freedom.

The development of ECHR

ECHR was the first fully developed human rights treaty and it has exercised very significant influence on other first generation human rights treaties as well as on many of the national constitutions drafted in the second half of the Twentieth Century. Its origins can be traced beyond Europe, to the United Nations. For practical purposes, the starting point is the Charter of the United Nations, signed on June 26, 1945. The Preamble states that the Peoples of the United Nations were determined:

"to reaffirm faith in fundamental human rights, in the dignity and worth of the human person, in the equal rights of men and women".

Article 1.3 states that one of the purposes of the UN is:

"To achieve international co-operation in solving international problems of an economic, social, cultural or humanitarian character, and in *promoting and encouraging respect for human rights and for fundamental freedoms without distinction as to race, sex, language or religion*" (emphasis added).

But work on this within the framework of the UN proceeded relatively slowly. Meanwhile, the Council of Europe was established in May 1949. (The Council of Europe is an entirely separate body from the European Union and the European Community, with a much wider membership and an entirely different role. These bodies must not be confused.)

A "Charter of Human Rights" had been contemplated specifically in the process which led to the establishment of the Council of Europe and Article 1.b of the Statute of the Council of Europe committed the Member States to, amongst other things, "the maintenance and further realisation of human rights and fundamental freedoms".

Article 3 of the Statute provided:

"Every Member...must accept the principles of the rule of law and of the enjoyment by all persons within its jurisdiction of human rights and fundamental freedoms".

In furtherance of these aspirations, the Council of Europe set up a Committee of Experts to prepare what was to become ECHR. It is clearly recorded in Government papers from the time that the first Part of ECHR, which contains the substantive rights, was based very closely indeed on texts proposed by the U.K. which were considered to be consistent with the existing state of English law.

ECHR was signed at Rome on November 4, 1950 and entered into force on September 3, 1953. After somewhat uncertain beginnings, ECHR has developed into what the late President of the Court called:

"a regional human rights protection system of unparalleled effectiveness. Its scope, its influence and the number of states that have agreed to abide by its standards have grown far beyond the most optimistic predictions of its founders. It is ... no exaggeration to say that, at least as far as the democratic protection of individuals and institutions is concerned, the Convention has become the single most important legal and political common denominator of the States of the Continent of Europe in the widest geographical sense" (*Ryssdal*, (1996)).

ECHR and E.C. law

It should be clear from what has just been said that ECHR has nothing to do with the European Community or the European Union. It is true that E.C. law uses ECHR as a source of law, but the relationship between ECHR and E.C. law is complex and need not be addressed here. None of what is dealt with in this book is within the category of European Community or European Union law. At the time of writing this book, the European Union Charter of Fundamental Rights was under negotiation, but neither its text nor its legal basis were settled. Although it might come in time to be an important source of human rights law in the United Kingdom, consideration of its provisions in this book would be highly speculative (and therefore unhelpful).

THE CONVENTION RIGHTS

The rights

ECHR sets out a number of rights. This book deals with those which are incorporated into United Kingdom law by the HRA. They are:

* Article 2: The right to life
* Article 3: The right not to be subjected to torture or to inhuman or degrading treatment or punishment
* Article 4: The right not to be held in slavery or to be required to perform forced labour
* Article 5: The right to liberty and security of person
* Article 6: The right to a fair hearing
* Article 7: The right not to be subjected to retrospective criminal-isation
* Article 8: The right to respect for private and family life, home and correspondence
* Article 9: The right to freedom of thought, conscience and religion
* Article 10: The right to freedom of expression
* Article 11: The right to freedom of assembly and association
* Article 12: The right to marry and found a family
* Article 14: The right not to be subject to discrimination in the enjoyment of the other Convention rights

There are in addition a number of Protocols to the Convention. The U.K. is not party to all of those Protocols, but the following rights in Protocols are incorporated by HRA:

- Protocol 1, Article 1: The right to peaceful enjoyment of possessions
- Protocol 1, Article 2: The right to education
- Protocol 1, Article 3: The right to free elections
- Protocol 6, Article 1: The abolition of the death penalty

In this book, as in HRA, the expression "the Convention rights" is used to refer to these rights.

Positive obligations

In general, the Convention rights are couched in negative terms. States undertake to refrain from doing certain things. But the Court has developed the concept of the "positive obligation". That means that although some of the provisions of the Convention are couched in negative language, they actually require the State to promote the enjoyment of the right concerned and not merely to refrain from interfering with it.

So, for example, *McCann, Farrell and Savage v. U.K.* (1995) and *Kaya v. Turkey* (1999) have made it clear that the right to life, guaranteed by Article 2, means that in a case where it is alleged or established that the right has been breached by police or security services the State is under a positive obligation to conduct a thorough, impartial and effective investigation and that the uncritical acceptance by the public prosecutor of police reports will fall far short of discharging that obligation.

But for our present purpose, *Johnston and Others v. Ireland* (1987) provides a still more helpful example. That case concerned, amongst other things, the position of the illegitimate child in Irish law. The Court held that, although Article 8 has as its essential object the protection of the individual against arbitrary interference by the public authorities with her private or family life, there may in addition be positive obligations inherent in an effective "respect" for family life. In particular, the State had an obligation to put in place arrangements so that the disabilities suffered by an illegitimate child (especially as regards her inheritance rights) were removed so as to respect her family relationship with her father.

THE EUROPEAN COURT OF HUMAN RIGHTS

The original arrangements

In its original form, ECHR established two organs for the enforcement of the rights which it guarantees, these being the European Commission of Human Rights ("the Commission") and the Court. Protocol 11 abolished the Commission and reconstructed the Court with effect from

November 1998, essentially because the structures could not cope with the large and increasing caseload. The Commission remained in being until November 1999 to deal with cases which were "on its books" in November 1998. The Court and the Commission are and were based in Strasbourg, where the Council of Europe also has its seat.

The Commission

The Commission (whose members had to be qualified for high judicial office in their home States) could receive applications from any person claiming to be the victim of a violation by one of the States party to ECHR of the rights set forth in the Convention which had made a declaration that it recognised the competence of the Commission to receive such applications. The U.K. recognised that competence with effect from January 1966. From this procedure is derived the term used for a person who asks the Court to consider a case. He or she is called "the applicant".

Having received an application, the Commission required first to consider its admissibility. Amongst a number of grounds on which the Commission could find an application inadmissible, the one which is of most practical importance for us is that which dealt with the application which was held to be manifestly ill founded. Commission decisions on this ground are published and often contain reasoning which is helpful in interpreting the Convention.

In relation to each petition, one member of the Commission was appointed *rapporteur* and he or she reported to the Commission as a whole. If the *rapporteur* reported that the petition was inadmissible, the Commission could accept that report and adopt a decision rejecting the petition, call for written submissions or hold an oral hearing. In the course of this the Commission was entitled to inquire into the facts. After however much of this procedure was relevant in a given case, the Commission adopted its decision on admissibility. It was obliged to give reasons for its decisions and these were published in the Council of Europe publication *Decisions and Reports* (usually abbreviated to "DR").

Where the Commission decided that a petition was admissible, it was obliged to attempt to mediate a so-called "friendly settlement". Whether or not it was successful in that attempt, the Commission prepared a report on the petition, which it transmitted to the State(s) concerned, the Committee of Ministers (which is one political forum of the Council of Europe) and the Secretary General of the Council of Europe for publication. Where friendly settlement was not achieved, the Commission expressed a view on whether the facts disclosed a breach of the Convention. The report, however, was not legally binding.

Once the Commission had transmitted its report, it or one of the States concerned was entitled to refer the matter to the Court within three months. If no such reference to the Court was made, the Committee of Ministers decided (by two-thirds majority) whether there had been a breach of the Convention. The decision of the Committee of Ministers is expressed in the form of a resolution.

The Court

Under the pre-November 1998 arrangements, each Member State of the Council of Europe supplied one judge to the Court. Cases were usually heard by a Chamber of nine judges. Where a case raised serious questions as to the interpretation of the Convention it might be dealt with by a Grand Chamber of 19 judges or even (occasionally) a Plenary Court. Proceedings before the Court were (and still are) predominantly written, with oral submissions being kept to a minimum. Once the judges had considered all the documents, a date was fixed for an oral hearing at which the Court was addressed by representatives of the State concerned, by representatives of the applicant and by representatives of the Commission.

Protocol 11 completely restructured the machinery of the Court. There are as many judges as there are parties to ECHR. Each judge is elected for six years. The Court sits in Committees of three judges, in Chambers of seven judges and in a Grand Chamber of 17 judges. Cases go first to a Committee and that Committee is entitled, by unanimous vote, to declare that a given application is inadmissible, provided that further examination of the case is not necessary. The criteria are essentially those previously applied by the Commission.

Where the Committee is unable to declare that an application is inadmissible a decision is taken on the admissibility and the merits of the application by a Chamber. Where an application is held to be admissible, the Court attempts to secure a friendly settlement. If that cannot be achieved, it proceeds to decide the case. Within three months of the decision of the Chamber a party can, in exceptional circumstances, request that the matter be referred to a Grand Chamber. A panel of five judges of the Grand Chamber will consider whether to grant that request. Where a case raises a serious question affecting the interpretation of the Convention, the Chamber may itself relinquish jurisdiction in favour of the Grand Chamber.

Where the Court finds that there has been a breach of the Convention and that the internal law of the State concerned allows only partial reparation for that, it is required to "afford just satisfaction" to the injured party. The Court has sometimes tended to hold that its decision that there has been a breach is sufficient satisfaction but where there is a demonstrable financial loss the Court is prepared to order the State to pay compensation. In *Saunders v. U.K.* (1996), having held that the applicant had been convicted and imprisoned after a trial which had been rendered unfair by the way in which the prosecution had used answers extracted from the applicant under compulsory powers which were not intended for use in a trial, the Court held that the finding of a violation constituted sufficient just satisfaction. By contrast, in *Pine Valley Developments Ltd v. Ireland* (1994), where the Court held that the applicants had been discriminated against in relation to planning legislation, to their quantifiable financial loss, a financial award was made.

The classes of case law

The classes of case law which arise out of all of this, and which are relevant to section 2 of HRA (discussed in Chapter 2) are as follows:

- *Judgement.* Final determination of a case by the Court.
- *Decision of the European Court of Human Rights.* A decision by a Chamber as to admissibility.
- *Declaration.* A declaration by a Committee of the Court that an application is inadmissible.
- *Advisory opinion.* Advisory opinions may be given by the Court in terms of Article 47, when the Committee of Ministers request advice as to the interpretation of the Convention or its Protocols. No such request has ever been made and, consequently, no such opinion has ever been given.
- *Opinion of the Commission.* The opinion which the Commission expressed as to whether or not there had been a breach of the Convention, once the application had been found to be admissible and attempts to arrive at a friendly settlement had failed.
- *Decision of the Commission.* A Commission decision on the admissibility of the application.
- *Decision of the Committee of Ministers.* A decision taken by the Committee of Ministers in cases in which the Commission had given its opinion on whether or not there had been a breach but which had not been referred to the Court.

INTERPRETATION OF THE CONVENTION

Introduction

The Convention is not a domestic statute and the European Court of Human Rights is not a domestic court. The Convention is a treaty and the Court is an international tribunal tasked with the interpretation of that Treaty. The Court itself summarised its task in this way:

"The Convention and the Protocol, which relate to matters normally falling within the domestic legal order of the Contracting States, are international instruments whose main purpose is to lay down certain international standards to be observed by the Contracting States in their relations with persons under their jurisdiction. The jurisdiction of the Court extends to all cases concerning the interpretation and application of those instruments" (*Belgian Linguistic Case (No. 1) (1979–80)*).

That means that the approach which the Court takes to the interpretation of the Convention is governed by international law and not by the principles of domestic statutory interpretation.

Detailed rules for the interpretation of treaties are provided by the Vienna Convention on the Interpretation of Treaties 1969. Those are the basis of the rules which are applied by the Court.

A number of principles are usually said to apply to the interpretation of ECHR, though there is very substantial overlap between them. They are as follows:

- No *quatrième* instance;
- Margin of appreciation;
- Autonomous meaning;
- Interpretation in good faith and in accordance with ordinary meaning;
- Object and purpose;
- Effective interpretation;
- Use of *travaux prépartatoires*
- Dynamic or evolutive interpretation; reliance on European national law standards.

No *quatrième* instance

As we have seen, the Court is an international tribunal tasked with the interpretation of a treaty. It is not a court of further appeal from national courts. One should never speak of "appealing to Strasbourg". The Court itself has consistently made a distinction between its own province and that of the national authorities. It says that it is not a Court of "*quatrième instance*"—that is, it will treat the national court's interpretation of national laws as conclusive. It is concerned only with the question whether the State has fulfilled its obligations in terms of the Convention. In *Saunders v. United Kingdom* (1996), for example, the Court held that the applicant's trial had been unfair but said in terms that it could not comment on whether the *outcome* of that trial had been correct or not. On that basis, it was held in *Locobail (U.K.) Ltd v. Waldorf Investment Corporation (No 4)* (2000) that a stay of proceedings in an English Court pending an application to Strasbourg would not be granted because the outcome in Strasbourg would not affect the outcome of the English proceedings.

Margin of Appreciation

It will also be helpful to understand the concept of the margin of appreciation, a principle most clearly enunciated in *Handyside v. U.K.* (1979–80), in which the Court said:

"By reason of their direct and continuous contact with the vital forces of their countries, state authorities are in principle in a better position than the international judge to give an opinion on the exact content of those requirements…"

In that case, the requirements concerned were those relating to the protection of public morals. What the Court was doing was refusing to intervene where they thought that the question of what was necessary in a democratic society was best decided by the national authorities in that society. However, they went on to say that Article 10.2, which deals with freedom of expression and with which they were concerned in that case does not give the contracting States:

"an unlimited margin of appreciation. The Court, which … is responsible for ensuring the observance of those States' engagements, is empowered to give the final ruling on whether a restriction…is reconcilable with freedom of expression as protected by Article 10".

To put it another way, the outer limits of what is acceptable are established by the Convention and policed by the Court. Within those limits, States may select their own boundaries according to national conditions and perceptions. Whilst the judges of the Court might not agree that what a State has done is entirely appropriate, provided it does not go outside the limits of the Convention, the Court will not interfere.

It should also be said that the width of the margin of appreciation varies from Article to Article. For example, in Article 10 there is a wide margin of appreciation, but in Article 3, which prohibits torture and inhuman or degrading treatment, there is virtually none. It is one thing to say that it is for individual States to decide, within broad limits, what aspects of public morality are to be restricted by the use of criminal sanctions which limit freedom of expression; it would be quite another to say that it is for individual states to decide whether or not to torture people.

Autonomous meaning
When the Convention uses a technical term, it does not necessarily use it in the same way as any given national legal system. Some terms are used by many national legal systems and their precise meanings vary from national system to national system. For example, the expression "criminal charge" is used in the Convention and also by most, if not all, legal systems; but the scope of the expression varies from system to system. Fixed penalties, for example, are characterised as criminal matters in some systems and as administrative in others. The need for consistency in meaning has led the Court to develop its own definitions of such words. This is the principle of "autonomous meaning". Its practical result is that, when reading cases from the Court, one must be careful not to assume that words which have a particular technical meaning in one's own legal system are necessarily used in precisely the same way by the Court.

Interpretation in good faith and in accordance with ordinary meaning
Article 31 of the 1969 Vienna Convention provides that:

"a treaty shall be interpreted in good faith in accordance with the ordinary meaning to be given to the terms of the treaty in their context and in the light of its object and purpose".

An example of the application of the "ordinary meaning" principle is to be found in *Luedicke, Belkacem and Koc v. Federal Republic of Germany* (1979–80). Each of the applicants was a foreign national with limited command of German who had been prosecuted and convicted of an offence in Germany and ordered to pay the costs of the proceedings, including the interpretation costs. Each applied to the Commission on the basis that the requirement to pay for the interpreter to whose services the Convention entitled them constituted a breach of Article 6.3(e).

The Court held that in interpreting Article 6.3(e) it would be guided by the Vienna Convention on the Law of Treaties 1969. In both French and English (the Court's two official languages) the terms "gratuitement" and "free", which Article 6.3(e) uses to describe the basis on which the interpreter's services are to be provided, are unqualified, denoting a once and for all exemption or exoneration. It had to be determined whether context and object and purpose negatived that literal interpretation. To read the Article as allowing the domestic court to require a person who has been convicted to meet interpretation costs would be to limit Article 6.3(e) in time and in practice to deny its benefit to a person who is eventually convicted. This might have implications for fair trial. The ordinary meaning of "gratuitement" and "free" is not contradicted by context or by object and purpose and the requirement to pay interpretation costs therefore amounted to a breach of the Convention.

The same point can be illustrated from *Golder v. United Kingdom* (1979–80), in which the Court was concerned with Article 6.1 of the Convention. So far as relevant, that provides that:

> "In the determination of his civil rights and obligations or of any criminal charge against him, everyone is entitled to a fair and public hearing in a reasonable time by an independent and impartial tribunal established by law..."

The facts in *Golder* were that a prisoner wished to sue a prison officer for libel in respect of a statement he made which alleged that the prisoner had participated in riot. As a result of that statement, sundry privileges were stopped, though formal disciplinary action was not taken against the prisoner. He was therefore unable to contest the allegation except by recourse to the civil courts. The prison governor stopped his letter to his solicitor, so preventing him from taking civil action. The Court held that Article 6 means what it says—everyone is entitled to a hearing to determine his civil rights. The U.K. Government had argued that Article 6 only applies where proceedings have already been commenced; in other words, that if there was a hearing it had to be fair but that there was no right to a hearing as such. The Court held that construction to be incorrect because it limited the words of the Convention in a way not justified by their ordinary meanings. By the action of the governor in stopping the letter, the applicant had been denied his right to a hearing to determine his civil rights, so that there was a breach of Article 6.

Object and purpose

Golder (1979–80) helps us with object and purpose as an interpretative tool as well. The Court took into account the fact that the Preamble to ECHR emphasises the "rule of law" as part of the object and purpose of the Convention and considered that the maintenance of the rule of law cannot be maintained if some classes of potential litigant are denied access to the courts. This consideration helped the Court to conclude that the U.K. was wrong in its argument that Article 6.1 did not give a right to a hearing as such.

Effective interpretation

The next principle is that of effective interpretation. This may best be demonstrated by *Artico v. Italy* (1981). In that case, the applicant had been convicted of fraud and obtained the appointment of a legal aid lawyer for his appeal. From the outset, that lawyer refused to act (on account of other commitments and the state of his health) and the applicant was, therefore, unrepresented at his appeal, which he lost.

Article 6.3(c) entitles everyone charged with a criminal offence to defend himself in person or through legal assistance of his own choosing or, if he has not sufficient means to pay for legal assistance, to be given it free when the interests of justice so require. The Italian Government argued that its responsibilities were fully discharged when the lawyer had been appointed but the Court was not prepared to accept that argument. It said that:

"the Convention is intended to guarantee not rights that are theoretical or illusory but rights that are practical and effective ... mere nomination does not ensure effective assistance."

It held that there had been a breach of the Convention.

Use of *travaux préparatatoires*

It is legitimate in treaty interpretation to refer to the record of the discussions which led to the treaty and these are published for ECHR. The Court sometimes uses this tool of interpretation but it does so most often to reinforce a conclusion which it has reached on other grounds. That being so, and since the relevant materials, although published, are not readily accessible, it is unlikely that there will be much occasion to refer to the *travaux* in domestic courts, albeit such reference is legitimate.

Dynamic or evolutive interpretation; reliance on European national law standards

Dynamic or evolutive interpretation and reliance on European national law standards are very closely related. The basic principle was stated in *Tyrer v. United Kingdom* (1979–80), in which the Court said that the Convention is "a living instrument which ... must be interpreted in the light of present day conditions".

On that basis, it held that judicial corporal punishment can no longer be regarded as consistent with the Article 3 prohibition on degrading punishment. However, there are limits to the principle of evolutive interpretation. In particular, it does not extend to creating a right not in the Convention in the first place (*Johnston v. Ireland* (1986)).

European national law standards are important to the Court in determining how to apply the principle of evolutive interpretation. If there is a developed, or clearly developing, consensus amongst Council of Europe Member States about what is or is not acceptable conduct, that will inform the approach of the Court. Sometimes comparative law techniques are applied to discover if there is such a consensus and, if so, what its content is. In other cases, such consensus may be identified from the existence of other, widely ratified, Council of Europe Conventions.

In *Tyrer v. United Kingdom* (1979–80), a comparative law approach permitted the Court to hold that there was an identifiable move away from judicial corporal punishment throughout Europe (except in Isle of Man). More recently, in *Selmouni v. France* (2000) the Court used this approach to hold that police mistreatment of the applicant, of a sort which would previously have been regarded as inhuman and degrading treatment, could now be regarded as torture.

The principles of interpretation in practice

It may be helpful to illustrate the way in which the Court combines several of the principles discussed in order to arrive at an interpretation of the Convention. This can be done by looking again at *Johnston v. Ireland* (1986).

There were three applicants. The first was a man who had married in 1952. He had parted from his wife in 1965. In 1976 he began to cohabit with the second applicant. The third applicant was their daughter, born in 1978. There was in Ireland a constitutional prohibition on the dissolution of marriage so that the first applicant could not divorce from his wife. He could not, therefore, marry the second applicant as a result of which she could not obtain the security provided by marriage in matters such as a right to be maintained by the first applicant and rights of succession on intestacy. Moreover, the third applicant was, as a result of the irregularity of her parents' relationship, illegitimate. This placed her in a less advantageous position as regards succession and maintenance rights against her father than would have been the case had she been legitimate and carried with it the risk of stigma if it became known.

They applied to the Commission, complaining of breaches of, amongst other things, Article 8 (the right to respect for family life) and Article 12 (the right to marry and found a family). They argued that the central issue was not whether the Convention guarantees the right to divorce but rather whether the fact that the first and second applicants were unable to marry each other was compatible with the rights to marry and to respect for family life enshrined in Articles 12 and 8.

The Court did not consider that the issues could be separated out in the watertight way urged by the applicants. In any society espousing monogamy it was inconceivable that the first applicant would be able to remarry before the dissolution of his existing marriage. The second applicant was not prevented in general from marrying but only from marrying the first applicant. The situation arose precisely because the first applicant could not obtain a divorce. Consequently, the case could not be examined in isolation from the problem of the non-availability of divorce. In order to determine whether the applicants could derive a right to divorce from Article 12 the Court had to seek to ascertain the ordinary meaning of the terms of that provision in their context and in the light of its object and purpose.

The ordinary meaning of the words "right to marry" are clear in the sense that they cover the formation of marital relationships but not their dissolution. This interpretation of Article 12 is consistent with what was revealed by the *travaux prépartatoires*. The provision was explained to the Consultative Assembly (which was part of the drafting process) as only guaranteeing the right to marry. Although the Convention fell to be interpreted in light of present-day conditions, the Court could not, by means of an evolutive interpretation derive from the Convention a right that was not included at the outset.

It was clear that the applicants constituted a family for the purposes of Article 8 and the question was whether an effective respect for their family life imposed on Ireland a positive obligation to introduce measures that would permit divorce. Although Article 8, with its somewhat vague notion of respect for family life, might appear to lend itself more readily to evolutive interpretation than does Article 12, the Convention must be read as a whole and the Court did not consider that a right to divorce, which it had found to be excluded from Article 12, could with consistency be derived from Article 8.

However, the third applicant's position was significantly less advantageous than that of a legitimate child. It was recorded in the preamble to the European Convention on the Legal Status of Children born out of Wedlock that "in a great number of Member States efforts have been or are being made to improve the legal status of children born out of wedlock by reducing the differences between their legal status and that of children born in wedlock". The Court could not but be influenced by these developments. Respect for family life implies an obligation for the State to act in a manner calculated to allow ties between near relatives to develop normally, which meant that the third applicant should be placed, legally and socially, in a position akin to that of a legitimate child.

Notwithstanding the wide margin of appreciation enjoyed by Ireland in this area, the absence of an appropriate legal regime reflecting the third applicant's natural family ties amounted to a failure to respect her family life. Moreover, the close relationship between the third applicant and her parents meant that there was a resultant failure to respect the family life of each of the latter. This did not amount to an indirect finding that the first applicant should be entitled to divorce and remarry—Ireland itself was proposing to improve the legal situation of illegitimate children whilst maintaining the constitutional prohibition on divorce.

---

2. HUMAN RIGHTS ACT 1998

INTRODUCTION

According to the White Paper, *Rights Brought Home*:
> "the essential feature of the Human Rights Bill is that the United Kingdom will not be bound to give effect to the Convention rights merely as a matter of international law, but will also give them further effect directly in our domestic law".

In Scotland, that is also the effect of section 57(2) of the Scotland Act 1998, which operates under substantial reference to HRA and which provides that:
> "A member of the Scottish Executive has no power to make any subordinate legislation, or to do any other act, so far as the legislation or act is incompatible with any of the Convention rights or with Community law".

Lord Justice-General Rodger has said, in *H.M. Advocate v. Montgomery and Coulter* (1999) that:
> "it would be wrong...to see the rights under the European Convention as somehow forming a wholly separate stream in our law; in truth they soak through and permeate the areas of our law in which they apply"

and that comment is as applicable to the effect of HRA as to the effect of section 57(2) the Scotland Act.

HUMAN RIGHTS ACT 1998, SECTION 6(1)

Section 6(1) of the Human Rights Act is the pivotal provision in that Act. It provides that "It is unlawful for a public authority to act in a way which is incompatible with a Convention right".

There are three things to be understood in this. They are:

- the meaning of "public authority";
- the meaning of "act"; and
- the effect of an act being unlawful in terms of the section.

Public authority

Section 6(3) provides that the expression "public authority" includes a court or tribunal and also "any person certain of whose functions are functions of a public nature". "Court" is not further defined but section 21(1) tells us that "tribunal" means "any tribunal in which legal proceedings may be brought".

The second part of the definition of a public authority is "any person certain of whose functions are functions of a public nature". At its core, this is straightforward enough. It plainly covers organisations such as the police, the fire service, NHS trusts, local authorities, the Procurator Fiscal Service, the Crown Prosecution Service and the Inland Revenue. Any number of other bodies which are obviously public could be identified. The more difficult questions are likely to arise at the margins. There was considerable concern on the part of the Christian churches, essentially because their role in solemnising marriages might have been thought to bring them within the definition of a public authority and if that meant that the Convention rights applied to their activities as a whole it might have meant that their internal affairs were to be subject to legal regulation in a way not previously known. If a secular court was asked to rule unlawful something which represented the outworking of a particular item of faith, that would have brought about a most difficult situation.

The involvement of the churches in marriage made the problem particularly acute for them; but similar questions might have arisen for other faiths and, indeed, for the charitable sector generally. Barnardos and other similar organisations, for example, have a number of joint projects with local authorities in relation to young offenders. Does that make them a public authority? Section 6(5) offers some assistance, by providing that, "in relation to a particular act, a person is not a public authority by virtue only of subsection (3)(b) if the nature of the act is private"; but this still leaves much scope for uncertainty.

Section 13 is intended to offer further comfort to religious organisations in particular. It provides:

"If a court's determination of any question arising under this Act might affect the exercise by a religious organisation (itself or its members collectively) of the Convention right to freedom of thought, conscience and religion, it must have particular regard to the importance of that right."

The Home Secretary, in the House of Commons, emphasised the requirement to have *particular* regard to the right to freedom of thought, conscience and religion and said that the:

"intention is to focus the courts' attention in any proceedings on the view generally held by the Church in question, and on its interest in protecting the integrity of the common faith of its members against attack, whether by outsiders or by individual dissidents" (*Hansard*, May 20, 1998).

This is consistent with Article 17 ECHR, which provides:

> "Nothing in this Convention may be interpreted as implying for any State, group or person any right to engage in any activity or perform any act aimed at the destruction of any of the rights and freedoms set forth herein or at their limitation to a greater extent than is provided for in the Convention."

It was the intention of those who drafted the Convention that persons of malicious intent should not be provided with a tool to subvert the rights which the Convention seeks to guarantee.

"Act"

The scope of the word "act" is reasonably straightforward. In its positive aspect, its meaning seems clear without elaboration. In addition, section 6(6) provides that "an act", for the purposes of the section, includes a failure to act. This brings us back to the concept of the positive obligation, which was discussed in Chapter 1. Public authorities can take no comfort from the fact that the Convention rights are couched in negative terms. Many of them involve positive obligations and if the authority does not discharge those obligations it will find itself in difficulties. We can take 2 (out of many potential) examples from the Convention case law.

The first example is *Plattform "Ärzte für das leben" v. Austria* (1991) in which the Court found that the Article 11 right to freedom of peaceful assembly involves a positive obligation on the State to take reasonable and appropriate measures to enable lawful demonstrations to proceed peacefully. In that case, it was held to have been sufficient for the police to interpose themselves between the applicants (an anti abortion organisation) who had been holding an open air religious service and those who were seeking to disrupt that service with loudspeakers and by throwing eggs. In the second example, however, the State was found to have failed in its positive obligation.

The case was *López Ostra v. Spain* (1994). A plant for the treatment of tannery waste was built on municipal land 12 metres away from the applicant's home. It began to operate without the requisite licence and its start-up released fumes, smells and contamination, which immediately caused health problems and nuisance to people living in the applicant's district. The local authority was substantially ineffective in dealing with the problem and the applicant and her family had to move house as a result.

The Court held that severe environmental pollution may affect individuals' well-being and prevent them from enjoying their homes in such a way as to affect their private and family life adversely even if it did not endanger their health. Although the local authority was not directly responsible for the emissions it could not be unaware that the environmental problems continued after the partial shutdown. The national authorities had not taken the positive measures necessary for protecting the applicant's right to respect for her home and for her private and family life and so there was a breach of Article 8.

It would seem, then, that one effect of section 6, HRA is to impose on public authorities a duty to use such means as are within their power to promote and protect the enjoyment of the Convention rights even where the interference or threatened interference comes from a private individual or corporation. It has to be stressed that, in *López Ostra*, the Court made it clear that the duty is not absolute. A balance has to be struck between the rights of the individuals concerned. What a public authority which has the power to intervene will not be able to do, however, is simply stand back and let the individuals fight the issue out between themselves.

The effect of unlawfulness

Section 7(1) and (6) provide that a person who claims that a public authority has acted (or proposes to act) in a way which is made unlawful by section 6(1) may bring proceedings against the authority under the Act in the appropriate court or tribunal or rely on the Convention right or rights concerned in any legal proceedings brought by or at the instigation of a public authority. This is subject to the qualification that the person concerned must be, in Convention terms, a victim of the unlawful act.

The Court held in *Klass v. Germany* (1979–80) that, if he or she is to be successful, an individual applicant will have to be able to claim to have been actually affected by the violation he alleges. The Convention does not permit individuals to complain against a law in the abstract simply because they feel that it contravenes the Convention. It is necessary that the law should have been applied to the detriment of the applicant; though the Court has held that a law may by itself violate the rights of an individual if the individual is directly affected by the law in the absence of any specific measure of implementation. An example of such a case is *Norris v. Ireland* (1991) in which a homosexual man was held to be entitled to complain about legislation which rendered persons carrying out homosexual acts liable to prosecution even though he had not himself been prosecuted and in practice the law was only actually operated where a minor was involved.

Subsection (5) provides that proceedings under subsection (1)(a) must be brought before the end of the period of one year beginning with the date on which the act complained of took place or such longer period as the court or tribunal considers equitable having regard to all the circumstances (subject to any rule imposing a stricter time limit in relation to the procedure in question).

Section 8(1) HRA provides that, in relation to any act (or proposed act) of a public authority which the court finds is (or would be) unlawful, it may grant such relief or remedy, or make such order, within its powers as it considers just and appropriate. This seems to make it clear that HRA is not creating any special procedures or new remedies. Rather, it is giving new grounds for existing remedies. It also puts certain limits on courts dealing with Convention rights based issues. In particular, subsection (3) provides that:

"No award of damages is to be made unless, taking account of all the circumstances of the case, including (a) any other relief or remedy granted, or order made, in relation to the act in question (by that or any other court), and (b) the consequences of any decision (of that or any other court) in respect of that act, the court is satisfied that the award is necessary to afford just satisfaction to the person in whose favour it is made."

As we saw in Chapter 1, in many cases the Court takes the view that a simple finding of a breach is sufficient "just satisfaction". This is reinforced by subsection (4), which tells us that, in determining whether to award damages or the amount of an award the national court must take into account the principles applied by the European Court of Human Rights in relation to the award of compensation under Article 41 of the Convention. Except where there is a quantifiable financial loss, the Court, if it awards compensation at all, tends to award sums which might almost be described as "token".

HUMAN RIGHTS ACT 1998, SECTION 6(2)

Introduction

Section 6(2) HRA qualifies subsection (1) by providing that it does not apply to an act if:

"(a) as the result of one or more provisions of primary legislation, the authority could not have acted differently; or (b) in the case of one or more provisions of, or made under, primary legislation which cannot be read or given effect in a way which is compatible with the Convention rights, the authority was acting so as to give effect to or enforce those provisions."

This brings us to the whole question of the relationship between Convention rights and Parliamentary sovereignty. It was the Government's clear policy, in enacting both the Human Rights Act and the Scotland Act, not to interfere with that doctrine. That policy has two manifestations which are of particular importance for this book. The first relates to the extent of, and limitations on, the requirement to interpret legislation so that it is consistent with the Convention rights; and the second relates to the limitation placed by section 6(2) on the rule that public authorities which act incompatibly with the Convention rights act unlawfully.

HUMAN RIGHTS ACT 1998, SECTIONS 2 AND 3

Section 3 HRA provides that:

"So far as it is possible to do so, primary legislation and subordinate legislation must be read and given effect in a way which is compatible with the Convention rights."

This makes an important change in the law as to the availability of ECHR for use in the interpretation of legislation in national courts. ECHR has hitherto been in the same position as any other unincorporated treaty—that is, as we saw in Chapter 1, it has been permissible to refer to it as an aid to the interpretation of legislation provision but only where the legislative provision to be interpreted was patently ambiguous. That limitation still applies to the use of all other human rights treaties, so that it would not, for example, be legitimate to invoke the International Covenant on Civil and Political Rights 1966 except where there is patent ambiguity in a statute. ECHR, however, has now been given special status. No matter what understanding the courts have had of a particular piece of legislation in the past and no matter what the most obvious meaning of the words of a statute might be, it is now the case that the statutory provision must be examined in the light of the Convention rights and the meaning selected which is compatible with those rights. As Lord Steyn (in 1998) has put it:

> "Traditionally the search has been for the one true meaning of a statute. Now the search will be for a possible meaning that would prevent the need for a declaration of incompatibility. The questions will be: (1) What meanings are the words capable of yielding? (2) And, critically, can the words be made to yield a sense consistent with Convention rights? In practical effect there will be a rebuttable presumption in favour of an interpretation consistent with Convention rights. Given the inherent ambiguity of language the presumption is likely to be a strong one."

Courts are not expected to interpret the Convention rights from scratch; indeed, that would be an entirely incorrect approach. The President of the Supreme Court of the Netherlands (himself a former Judge of the Court) has written that the:

> "highly abstract form in which the norms enshrined in the ECHR are worded offers little assistance when it comes to working out what a particular provision implies in a specific case" (Martins, 1998).

Section 2(1) HRA provides that:

> "a court or tribunal determining a question which has arisen under the Act in connection with a Convention right must take into account any—
>
> (a) judgement, decision, declaration or advisory opinion of the European Court of Human Rights;
>
> (b) opinion of the Commission given in a report adopted under Article 31 of the Convention;
>
> (c) decision of the Commission in connection with Article 26 or 27(2) of the Convention; or
>
> (d) decision of the Committee of Ministers taken under Article 46 of the Convention,

whenever made or given, so far as, in the opinion of the court or tribunal, it is relevant to the proceedings in which that question arises".

This recognises that the use of the case law of the Court and the Commission will be essential. The obligation is, however, only to take that case law into account, not to treat it as binding. The Lord Chancellor explained at Report in the House of Lords that the Convention itself has no rule of precedent and went on to say that:

> "should a United Kingdom court ever have a case before it which is a precise mirror of one that has been previously been considered by the European Court of Human Rights, which I doubt, it may be appropriate for it to apply the European Court's findings directly to that case; but...the courts will often be faced with cases that involve factors specific to the United Kingdom which distinguish them from cases considered by the European court" (*Hansard*, January 19, 1998).

In such cases, he said, and also in cases where the Strasbourg jurisprudence is out of date, it was important that U.K. courts should have the flexibility and discretion to develop the law.

Declarations of incompatibility

The acid test will come when a court finds it impossible to find an interpretation of a piece of legislation which is consistent with the Convention rights. The Government's answer was clear. At Second Reading of the Human Rights Bill in the House of Lords, the Lord Chancellor said that "the Bill does not allow the courts to set aside or ignore Acts of Parliament" and that section 3 "preserves the effect of primary legislation which is incompatible with the Convention" (*Hansard*, November 3, 1997).

Later in the same debate, he said that the intention of the legislation was to maximise the protection to individuals "while retaining the fundamental principle of Parliamentary sovereignty". The remedy provided for the situation in which a court cannot find a way to construe legislation compatibly with the Convention rights is the declaration of incompatibility, which will not affect the validity, continuing operation or enforcement of the provision in respect of which it is given and which will not bind the parties to the proceedings in which it is made. Such a declaration might well prompt the Government to make legislative change but will not oblige it to do so.

A declaration of incompatibility can only be made, in terms of section 4(5), by superior courts—in particular:

- the House of Lords;
- the Judicial Committee of the Privy Council;
- the Courts-Martial Appeal Court;
- the High Court of Justiciary sitting otherwise than as a trial court;
- the Court of Session;

- the High Court;
- the Court of Appeal.

---

3. RIGHT TO LIFE (ARTICLE 2)

INTRODUCTION

Article 2 provides:
> "1. Everyone's right to life shall be protected by law. No one shall be deprived of his life intentionally save in the execution of a sentence of a court following his conviction of a crime for which this penalty is provided by law.
>
> 2. Deprivation of life shall not be regarded as inflicted in contravention of this Article when it results from the use of force which is no more than absolutely necessary:
> (a) in defence of any person from unlawful violence;
> (b) in order to effect a lawful arrest or to prevent the escape of a person lawfully detained;
> (c) in action lawfully taken for the purpose of quelling a riot or insurrection".

Paragraph 1 states the right:
> "Everyone's right to life shall be protected by law. No-one shall be deprived of his life intentionally..."

Paragraph 2 explains and qualifies this by setting out 3 sets of circumstances in which deprivation of life is not within the ambit of the Article. The second part of paragraph 1 states the permitted exception. Finally, we should note, Article 2 has been held to give rise to positive obligations, which are considered below.

THE SCOPE OF THE RIGHT

The most obvious application of Article 2 is to deliberate killing by state officials. In fact, however, it is not so restricted. There need not be an intention to kill. In *Stewart v. United Kingdom* (1984), the Commission held that Article 2 was apt to cover the situation in which a soldier firing a rubber bullet at the legs of a rioter in Belfast missed (because he was hit by a brick as he pulled the trigger) and the projectile struck a 12 year old boy on the head, killing him. There was no question of the boy having been killed deliberately.

Nor is it necessary for the victim to actually die before Article 2 issues can arise. It is enough if his life is put at material risk. In *Yaça v. Turkey* (1999) the applicant was shot by two unknown assailants. He survived and claimed that he had been shot by state officials because of his involvement in the sale of a pro-Kurdish newspaper. His uncle was shot and killed a few weeks later. The case was dealt with ultimately on the basis of the State's positive obligation to investigate but the starting point was that Article 2 was applicable in the case of the applicant even though he did not die.

Because it is well recognised that the Convention is a "living instrument", to be interpreted evolutively (as described in Chapter 1), it is common for those who feel that there is a gap in the law, for pressure groups and for those with concerns about particular aspects of the law to seek to use the Convention to fill the perceived gap or as a vehicle for the advancement of their chosen cause or position. This often involves arguments which seek to invest a Convention right with a rather wide meaning. Article 2 has been the subject of its share of such attention.

In *Taylor Family v. United Kingdom* (1994) the Commission refused to consider the funding of the Health Service under the head of Article 2 (it having been argued that financial cut backs had led to inadequate supervision which had allowed a nurse to murder babies in hospital) and in *Association X v. United Kingdom* (1978) it concluded that, although a small proportion of children who had received a particular vaccination had suffered brain damage or death, overall the system for ensuring the safety of the vaccinations was a responsible one and properly administered which complied with Article 2.

Questions have been raised about the effect of Article 2 in relation to abortion and euthanasia. These questions have not yet received any clear answers, not least because the absence of a European consensus on these subjects makes it difficult for the Court to interpret Article 2 in light of any relevant common European practice. As regards abortion, in *Open Door Counselling and Dublin Well Woman v. Ireland* (1992), which related to an injunction restraining the applicants from giving information about abortion, the majority of the judges did not address the question whether Article 2 protects the child *in utero* but the dissenting minority said clearly that it does. In *Paton v. United Kingdom* (1981) the Commission held that there was no breach of Article 2 in the case of an abortion to protect the health of the mother, carried out at a relatively early stage of pregnancy, but did not explain whether that was because the unborn child is not protected by Article 2 or whether it was because the right had to be balanced against other rights of the mother under the Convention. As regards euthanasia, the opportunity to clarify the application of Article 2 was missed—or avoided—in *D. v. United Kingdom* (1997) when the Court dealt with the case under Article 3 and declined to rule substantively on the Article 2 issue.

"Absolutely necessary"

Paragraph 2 takes a killing outside the scope of Article 2 where it is in defence of any person from unlawful violence, in order to effect a lawful arrest or to prevent the escape of a person lawfully detained or in action lawfully taken for the purpose of quelling a riot or insurrection. These exceptions have it in common that the force used must be "absolutely necessary".

In *McCann v. United Kingdom* (1995), an SAS unit shot IRA members who were in Gibraltar, according to intelligence, in order to plant a bomb. The Court found against the State because, although the soldiers who shot the terrorist suspects in that case had acted reasonably in opening fire when they thought a bomb was about to be detonated, those organising the counter terrorist operation could have avoided the possibility of such shooting by choosing to have the suspects detained at an earlier stage.

By contrast, in *Andronicou and Constantinou v. Cyprus* (1997) the Court held that the use of lethal force had been absolutely necessary in a siege where a man armed with a shotgun held a hostage and the authorities tried everything they could up to the deadline set by the man before storming the flat.

Other cases on the same point include *Wolfgram v. FRG* (1986), in which the Commission held that police officers had been entitled to open fire when a suspect threw a grenade at them, and *Diaz Ruano v. Spain* (1994), in which (with some dissent) the Commission held that when a man being interviewed by the police seized one officer's gun and shot at the other officer the officer who had been shot at was entitled to fire back, killing the man.

Specified objectives

Granted that the force used is no more than absolutely necessary, it must still pursue one of the specified objectives in paragraph 2 which, the Commission said in *Stewart*, are exhaustive and must be interpreted narrowly. *McCann, Andronicou, Wolfgram* and *Diaz Ruano* are all examples of the use of force in defence against unlawful violence and the way in which the Court has handled that issue.

There have been no cases which clearly exemplify the justified use of lethal force in the course of an arrest. *Aytekin v. Turkey* (1997) is an example of the *unjustified* use of force in such a case—the Commission considered that there was a breach of Article 2 where, with the intention of stopping a car which was proceeding slowly through a check point in such a way as to pose no risk of harm to those manning the checkpoint, a police officer shot and killed the driver.

In *Kelly v. United Kingdom* (1993) the use of lethal force at a checkpoint was held to have been justified but that was in relation to a vehicle which was being driven so aggressively as to put the soldiers manning the checkpoint at risk, so as to bring the case within the defence against unlawful violence exception.

Stewart is an example of the third category. The Commission was not impressed with the argument made by the applicant that 150 people throwing missiles at a patrol of soldiers did not constitute a riot and held that an accidental death caused by the use of rubber bullets to try to quell that riot did amount to action lawfully taken for that purpose.

Capital punishment

The specific exception provided for by Article 2.1 is for capital punishment. As regards the United Kingdom, this will not arise directly because the law no longer provides for the death penalty and the United Kingdom has acceded to Protocol 6 ECHR, paragraph 1 of which provides that "The death penalty shall be abolished. No-one shall be condemned to such a penalty or executed". By Schedule 1 to HRA, this is one of the Convention rights. The point might, however, arise indirectly. It was held by the Court in *Kirkwood v. United Kingdom* (1984) and *Soering v. United Kingdom* (1989) that extradition to a country where the applicant might face the death penalty does not as such breach the Convention though there might be a breach of Article 3 if the conditions likely to be applied to the applicant in the country requesting extradition are sufficiently bad. We shall look at that in more detail in the next chapter.

As regards Article 2, it has to be noted that the United Kingdom was not at the time of those cases a party to Protocol 6. It might be that accession to that Protocol could in future be argued to have changed the basis on which such cases are to be decided so that extradition to a country where the death penalty might follow would breach Article 2; but it must be emphasised that at present this is speculative.

Positive obligation

There are 2 aspects to the positive obligation which should take our attention. The first of these is that in the case of a death as a result of the activities of state officials, there must be a thorough and impartial investigation, usually in public. The Court made that point in *McCann* and commented favourably on the inquest proceedings which had taken place. By contrast, in *Yaça* the Court held that the mere fact that the authorities had been informed of the murder of the applicant's uncle had given rise to an obligation under Article 2 to carry out an effective investigation. The Turkish Government had provided no concrete information on the state of progress of the investigations which, more than five years after the events, did not appear to have produced any tangible result or have made any credible headway. In consequence there had been a violation of Article 2.

Secondly, there is the question of the extent to which the police should respond to a threat to the life of an individual. This has been addressed in the case of *Osman v. United Kingdom* (2000) in which a teacher, who had formed an irrational and entirely inappropriate attachment to one of his pupils, committed a number of minor offences of vandalism in furtherance of that attachment and then went on to kill the boy's father and another person. The family sought to sue the police for failing to protect them adequately and the Court said, in this context, that where the authorities know of a real and immediate threat to a person's life there is an obligation to take preventive operational measures to protect that person. The Court stressed, however, that the obligation is not to be interpreted so as to impose an impossible or disproportionate burden on the authorities. It is, for example, clear that the authorities are not required to maintain a bodyguard where the risk is a general one, such as that associated with holding public office in Ireland at the height of the troubles (*W v. United Kingdom* (1983)).

---

4. PROHIBITION OF TORTURE (ARTICLE 3)

INTRODUCTION

Article 3 is in uncompromising and unqualified terms:
> "No one shall be subjected to torture or to inhuman or degrading treatment or punishment."

It will be seen that this identifies three species of mistreatment:

- torture;
- inhuman treatment or punishment; and
- degrading treatment or punishment.

These things are not synonymous and the Court does not treat every unwarranted application of violence as a breach of Article 3. In the *Greek Interstate Case* (1969) the Commission distinguished acts prohibited by Article 3 from what it called a "certain roughness of treatment" which might take the form of slaps or blows of the hand on the face or the head. The Commission considered that, although such treatment is to be condemned on moral grounds (and might in some circumstances amount to a breach of Article 8) it did not amount to a breach of Article 3. However, the Court did make it clear, in *Ribitsch v. Austria* (1996) that, in respect of a person deprived of his liberty, any use of physical force which has not been made strictly necessary by his own conduct diminishes human dignity and is in principle an infringement of the right set forth in Article 3 of the Convention. The requirements of an investigation and the undeniable difficulties inherent in the fight against crime could not, the Court said, justify placing limits on the protection to be afforded in respect of the physical integrity of individuals.

TORTURE

Torture was defined in *Ireland v. United Kingdom* (1979–80) as "deliberate inhuman treatment causing *very serious and cruel* suffering" (emphasis added).

A very clear example of the kind of conduct which will amount to torture is to be found in *Aydin v. Turkey* (1998). In that case, the applicant was a 17 year old Turkish citizen of Kurdish origin. She was detained and taken to the local police headquarters. There she was blindfolded, beaten, stripped, placed inside a tyre and sprayed with high-pressure water, and raped. It appeared probable that the applicant was subjected to such treatment because it was suspected that she or other members of her family had collaborated with Kurdish separatists.

The Court pointed out that Article 3 of the Convention enshrines one of the fundamental values of democratic societies and as such it prohibits in absolute terms torture or inhuman or degrading treatment or punishment. It went on to say that, in order to determine whether any particular form of ill-treatment should be qualified as torture, regard must be had to the distinction drawn in Article 3 between this notion and that of inhuman treatment or degrading treatment. This distinction had been embodied in the Convention to allow the special stigma of "torture" to attach only to deliberate inhuman treatment causing very serious and cruel suffering. The Court was satisfied that the accumulation of acts of physical and mental violence inflicted on the applicant and the especially cruel act of rape to which she was subjected amounted to torture in breach of Article 3.

The threshold for what will constitute very serious and cruel suffering is not fixed. In *Selmouni v. France* (2000), the applicant had been arrested and questioned over several days in connection with alleged drug-trafficking. Subsequent medical examination found that he presented "lesions of traumatic origin on his skin that were sustained at a time which corresponds to the period of police custody". Police officers were subsequently convicted of assaulting him. The Court reiterated that it must have regard to the distinction between the concept of torture and that of inhuman or degrading treatment. It was clear that the treatment to which Selmouni had been subjected was sufficiently serious to be characterised as inhuman and degrading but not that it was serious enough to amount to torture. The Court recalled that the Convention is a "living instrument which must be interpreted in the light of present-day conditions". It said that certain acts which were classified in the past as "inhuman and degrading treatment" as opposed to "torture" could be classified differently in future. It took the view that the increasingly high standard being required in the area of the protection of human rights and fundamental liberties correspondingly and inevitably requires greater firmness in assessing breaches of the fundamental values of democratic societies. It found that the conduct to which Selmouni had been subjected amounted to torture.

In determining whether conduct amounts to torture, the Court lays some emphasis on the purpose for which violence is used. If that purpose is to obtain information or a confession from a person suspected of involvement in crime, the Court is more likely to regard the conduct as amounting to torture. That motive was significant in *Ireland v. United Kingdom* (1979–80) and also in *Dikme v. Turkey* (2000). In *Dikme*, a suspect was interrogated with considerable brutality and electrodes were applied to his feet, ears and genitals. The Court considered that this treatment had been inflicted on him intentionally by servants of the State in the performance of their duties with the aim of extracting from him confessions or information about offences. That being so, taking all these acts of violence against the applicant's person together, and having regard to the length of time for which they had lasted and their purpose, the Court considered they had been particularly serious and cruel, so that they must have caused Dikme "acute" pain and suffering. They accordingly warranted the classification of torture within the meaning of Art. 3.

INHUMAN TREATMENT

In *Ireland v. United Kingdom*, the treatment complained of included keeping detainees' heads covered by a hood, subjecting them to continuous loud noise, depriving them of sleep, depriving them of food and making them stand against a wall for hours at a time with their feet widely separated. This, it was held, was inhuman treatment but did not occasion suffering of the particular intensity and cruelty implied by the word "torture".

DEGRADING TREATMENT

In *Tyrer v. United Kingdom* (1979–80), the Court explained that, for a punishment to be "degrading" and in breach of Article 3, the humiliation or debasement involved must attain a particular level and must in any event be other than the usual element of humiliation involved in judicial punishment. The assessment is relative and depends on all the circumstances and, in particular, on the nature and context of the punishment itself and the manner and method of its execution. That case established that judicial corporal punishment (*i.e.* that inflicted by the State) is likely to constitute degrading treatment.

A number of cases have established that whether or not corporal punishment in schools will reach the threshold for Article 3 will depend on the circumstances of each particular case. The threat of the tawse was not degrading in Cowdenbeath in 1982 (in part, it seems, because the culture was such that almost everybody got the tawse at some stage) (*Campbell and Cosans v. United Kingdom* (1982)) and the use of a rubber-soled gym shoe on a boy of primary school age was not degrading in 1993 (*Costello Roberts v. United Kingdom* (1995)). However, a caning preceded by a run up and which inflicted injury was degrading (*Y v. United Kingdom* (1994)) as was the caning on the hand of a 16 year old girl by a male teacher in the presence of another male teacher (*Warwick v. United Kingdom* (1986)).

BURDEN OF PROOF

The Court held in *Ribitsch* and again in *Selmouni* that where an individual is taken into police custody in good health but is found to be injured at the time of release, it is incumbent on the State to provide a plausible explanation of how those injuries were caused, failing which a clear issue arises under Article 3 of the Convention. Absent an innocent explanation for Selmouni's injuries, the State had prima facie failed to meet its obligation under Article 3 of the Convention to ensure that he was not subjected to torture or to inhuman or degrading treatment.

ARTICLE 3 AND EXTRADITION OR DEPORTATION

There is, as the Court said in *Soering v. United Kingdom* (1989), no right in ECHR not to be extradited. Indeed, there is only one reference to extradition in ECHR (Article 5.1(f)) and that reference does not create a right. On the contrary, it qualifies the Article 5 right to liberty and security of person by specifying detention with a view to extradition as one of the permitted exceptions to the rule that persons are not to be deprived of their liberty. But, as the Court went on to say in *Soering*:

"in so far as a measure of extradition has consequences adversely affecting the enjoyment of a Convention right it may, assuming the consequences are not too remote, attract the obligations of a Contracting State under the relevant Convention guarantee".

In particular, in *Soering* and certain other cases, the Court has held that it would be a breach of Article 3 to extradite or deport someone to a jurisdiction where he or she is likely to be subject to treatment which, if it occurred in the respondent State, would breach that Article. In *Soering,* the Court said that Article 3 enshrines one of the fundamental values of the democratic societies making up the Council of Europe and that it would not be compatible with the underlying values of the Convention if a Contracting State were knowingly to surrender a fugitive to another State where there were substantial grounds for believing that he would be in danger of being subjected to torture, however heinous the crime allegedly committed. In the Court's view, this inherent obligation not to extradite also extended to cases in which the fugitive would be faced in the receiving State by a real risk of exposure to inhuman or degrading treatment or punishment proscribed by Article 3. The Secretary of State's decision to extradite the applicant to Virginia would, if implemented, give rise to a breach of Article 3 because the applicant might there be subject to the "death row phenomenon", spending many years in a condemned cell awaiting execution.

Jabardi v. Turkey (2000) also concerned Article 3. The applicant was an Iranian woman who had fallen in love with a man whose family was opposed to their marriage. He married another woman but they continued to see each other and to have sexual intercourse. They were discovered and arrested for adultery, the penalty for which in Iran is death by stoning or flogging.

Understandably enough when the applicant was fortunate enough to be set at liberty through the intervention of relatives, she fled the country and entered Turkey illegally. She tried to fly to Canada via France but the French authorities discovered that she had a forged passport and sent her back to Istanbul. There she was arrested on the ground that she had entered Turkey using a forged passport. No charges were brought against her on account of the forged passport but she was ordered to be deported. The applicant subsequently lodged an asylum request, which was rejected by the Turkish authorities but she was granted refugee status by the United Nations High Commission for Refugees branch office in Ankara. Nevertheless, the Ankara Administrative Court dismissed the applicant's petition against the implementation of her deportation on the grounds that there was no need to suspend it since it was not tainted with any obvious illegality and its implementation would not cause irreparable harm to the applicant.

She applied to the Court, which noted that the Ankara Administrative Court had limited itself to the issue of the formal legality of the applicant's deportation rather than the more compelling question of the substance of her fears. The Court attached weight to the fact that the UNHCR, having interviewed the applicant, concluded that her fears were credible. The Court was not persuaded either that the situation in the applicant's country of origin has evolved to the extent that adulterous behaviour is no longer considered a reprehensible affront to Islamic law. In this connection, it took judicial notice of recent surveys of the current situation in Iran and noted that punishment of adultery by stoning still remains on the statute book and may be resorted to by the authorities. Having regard to these considerations, the Court found it substantiated that there was a real risk of the applicant being subjected to treatment contrary to Article 3 if returned to Iran and accordingly her deportation, if executed, would give rise to a violation of Article 3.

---

5. RIGHT TO LIBERTY (ARTICLE 5)

INTRODUCTION

Article 5 provides:

"1. Everyone has the right to liberty and security of person. No one shall be deprived of his liberty save in the following cases and in accordance with a procedure prescribed by law:
   a. the lawful detention of a person after conviction by a competent court;
   b. the lawful arrest or detention of a person for non-compliance with the lawful order of a court or in order to secure the fulfilment of any obligation prescribed by law;
   c. the lawful arrest or detention of a person effected for the purpose of bringing him before the competent legal authority on reasonable suspicion of having committed an offen-

ce or when it is reasonably considered necessary to prevent
his committing an offence or fleeing after having done so;

d. the detention of a minor by lawful order for the purpose of
    educational supervision or his lawful detention for the
    purpose of bringing him before the competent legal
    authority;

e. the lawful detention of persons for the prevention of the
    spreading of infectious diseases, of persons of unsound
    mind, alcoholics or drug addicts or vagrants;

f. the lawful arrest or detention of a person to prevent his
    effecting an unauthorised entry into the country or of a
    person against whom action is being taken with a view to
    deportation or extradition.

2. Everyone who is arrested shall be informed promptly, in a
language which he understands, of the reasons for his arrest and of
any charge against him.

3. Everyone arrested or detained in accordance with the
provisions of paragraph 1.c of this article shall be brought promptly
before a judge or other officer authorised by law to exercise judicial
power and shall be entitled to trial within a reasonable time or to
release pending trial. Release may be conditioned by guarantees to
appear for trial.

4. Everyone who is deprived of his liberty by arrest or detention
shall be entitled to take proceedings by which the lawfulness of his
detention shall be decided speedily by a court and his release
ordered if the detention is not lawful.

5. Everyone who has been the victim of arrest or detention in
contravention of the provisions of this article ·shall have an
enforceable right to compensation."

As can be seen, Article 5.1 begins by stating the general right:
"Everyone has the right to liberty and security of person". It then states
the permitted exceptions to the right:

"No one shall be deprived of his liberty save in the following
cases and in accordance with a procedure prescribed by law".

Six subparagraphs then set out the cases in which deprivation of liberty
is permitted. They are exhaustive and fall to be construed narrowly
(*Monnell and Morris v. United Kingdom* (1987)). If a deprivation of
liberty cannot be brought within one of these six cases, it necessarily
involves a breach of Article 5.1 (*Ciulla v. Italy* (1991)). Given a
deprivation of liberty for the purposes of Article 5, the authority
responsible for that deprivation must, if it is to avoid a finding of breach,
bring the case within one of the permitted exceptions to the right. It
should be noted, however, that the mere fact that the decision to deprive
a person of his or her liberty is overturned on appeal will not by itself
establish a breach of Article 5.1 (*Perks and others v. United Kingdom*
(1999)).

DEPRIVATION OF LIBERTY

The first question in relation to Article 5 will always be whether there has been a deprivation of liberty. This concept has been contrasted with the more limited idea of restrictions on freedom of movement. In *Engel v. The Netherlands* (1979–80), the confining of military personnel to barracks did not amount to a deprivation of liberty but locking them up did. It is not, however, necessary that the person concerned should have been arrested or detained formally for there to be a deprivation of liberty. The concept includes any element of compulsion restricting a person to a particular location. So the confinement of asylum seekers "air-side" at an airport (*Amuur v. France* (1996)) and the confinement to an hotel of sect members undergoing deprogramming (*Riera–Blume and Others v. Spain* (1999)) have both constituted deprivation of liberty for the purposes of Article 5.

PROCEDURE PRESCRIBED BY LAW

The Court has said in cases such as *Winterwerp v. The Netherlands* (1980) and *Steel and others v. United Kingdom* (1999) that there must be full compliance with domestic law and also that the applicable domestic law be formulated with sufficient precision to allow the citizen—if need be with legal advice—to foresee to a reasonable degree the legal consequences of any given action. It has been held in other contexts under the Convention that common law rules are in principle adequate to satisfy this requirement (*e.g. Sunday Times v. United Kingdom* (1980) and *C.R. v. United Kingdom; S.W. v. United Kingdom* (1995)).

It is important to recognise that lawfulness in domestic law is not by itself decisive. In *Erkalo v. The Netherlands* (1997) the application by the authorities to extend the period during which the applicant was detained compulsorily in a mental hospital was miss-filed by the court and not dealt with until well after the authority to so detain him had expired. Although the national court agreed with the applicant's submission that the application was out of time and therefore in principle no longer admissible, it nonetheless declined to order his release, considering that it was imperative in the public interest that he remain in detention. No appeal lay against this decision.

The Court held that the lawfulness of the extension of the applicant's placement under domestic law is not in itself decisive. It must also be established that his detention during the period under consideration was in conformity with the purpose of Article 5.1 of the Convention, namely to protect individuals from arbitrariness. Although all the relevant authorities had been aware that the applicant's placement was due to expire, none of them took any steps to verify whether the request had been received at the registry of the national court and whether a date had been fixed for a hearing on the request. The detention of the applicant after expiry of the original order was not compatible with the purpose of Article 5 and was for that reason unlawful.

THE SIX CASES

Conviction

The first case in which deprivation of liberty is permitted under the Convention is, in terms of Article 5.1(a) the lawful detention of a person after conviction by a competent court. This, of course, deals with a sentence of imprisonment and, although it is straightforward for the most part, there have been questions about what constitutes a "court" for the purposes of subparagraph (a) and what connection there has to be between the conviction and the detention to satisfy the subparagraph.

The word "court" was considered in *De Wilde, Ooms and Versyp v. Belgium* (1979–80), in which the Court said that the word "court" implies common elements where it is used in Articles 2.1, 5.1(a) and (b), 5.4 and 6.1. Those elements are:

• independence of the executive and of the parties to the case; and
• the guarantees of judicial procedure.

In *De Wilde*, the procedure in question was that for the detention of vagrants and the Belgian authorities explained that the Code of Criminal Procedure did not apply, even though the consequence of the proceedings was detention which lasted, in the case of one of the applicants, for 21 months. The Court held, therefore, that the Police Court in which the detention was ordered did not satisfy the Convention definition of a "court".

The question of the connection between the conviction and the detention was considered in *Weeks v. United Kingdom* (1987). The applicant had been sentenced to life imprisonment for armed robbery. He was released on licence three times but each time his licence was revoked. He argued that his detention following revocation did not amount to lawful detention after conviction by a competent court. The Court, however, noted that the possibility of revocation was inherent in the concept of the life sentence and that each revocation had been triggered by conduct on the part of the applicant which had given cause for concern (especially where he had been assessed, in connection with the imposition of the sentence, as dangerous). The Court therefore found sufficient connection between the sentence and the revocations.

Court orders and obligations prescribed by law

Article 5.1(b) permits the arrest or detention of a person in 2 situations:

• for non compliance with the lawful order of a court;
• to secure the fulfilment of any obligation prescribed by law.

The first part of this is concerned with the sort of thing that could lead to a finding of contempt of court. It has, for example, been held to apply to failure to make a declaration of assets ordered by a court (*X. v. F.R.G.* (1983)). It does not, however, permit imprisonment for failure to comply with a contractual obligation (for example, failure to pay a debt even after litigation in which the creditor has been successful). Such imprisonment is specifically excluded by the Fourth Protocol to ECHR and although the U.K. is not a party to that Protocol the commentators agree that this does not mean that imprisonment for debt is permitted in the U.K. by Article 5.1(b). Imprisonment in respect of failure to pay a fine, on the other hand, *is* permitted (*Airey v. Ireland* (1977)).

In *Engel and Others v. The Netherlands* (1979–80), the Court explained that the second leg, permitting detention to secure the fulfilment of any obligation prescribed by law, concerns cases:

> "where the law permits the detention of a person to compel him to fulfil a specific and concrete obligation which he has until then failed to satisfy"

but not internment meant to compel a citizen to discharge his general duty of obedience to the law. Examples of obligations which are relevant to Article 5.1(b) have included an obligation to make customs or tax returns (*McVeigh, O'Neill and Evans v. United Kingdom* (1981)).

Suspicion of crime

Article 5.1(c) permits:

> "the lawful arrest or detention of a person effected for the purpose of bringing him before the competent legal authority on reasonable suspicion of having committed an offence or when it is reasonably considered necessary to prevent his committing an offence or fleeing having done so."

The preventative arrest which this contemplates and the possibility of arrest to prevent flight have hardly been addressed by the Strasbourg authorities (though in *Lukanov v. Bulgaria* (1997) the Commission held that the state's right to arrest to prevent flight depends on the existence of reasonable suspicion that the person concerned has in fact committed an offence). Deprivation of liberty to prevent flight following the commission of an offence is, however, very common.

Taken literally, the requirement that deprivation of liberty should have the purpose of placing the person detained before the court would mean that deprivation of liberty would breach the Convention unless that person was both kept in custody and presented to the court. In other words, the police and the prosecutor could not safely decide to liberate the accused having once arrested him. In *Brogan v. United Kingdom* (1989), however, the Court declined to take that approach. It said that Article 5.1(c) does not presuppose that the police should have obtained sufficient evidence to bring charges and proceeded on the basis that it is legitimate to detain so as to further an investigation and that, if sufficient evidence was obtained during that investigation, no doubt the person detained would be put before the court.

In *Brogan* the persons detained were not in fact placed before the court (because there was insufficient evidence after investigation). The Court did not find a breach of the Convention in that regard.

Reasonable suspicion refers to the existence of facts or information that would satisfy an independent observer that the person concerned might have committed the offence (*Fox, Campbell and Hartley v. United Kingdom* (1990)) but full proof is not necessary (*X v. Austria* (1989)) (otherwise *Brogan* could not have been decided as it was).

Detention of minors

Article 5.1(d) permits the detention of a minor for 2 purposes:

* educational supervision; or
* in order to bring him before the competent legal authority.

Neither of these has been very fully considered by the Commission or the Court. So far as educational supervision goes, the clearest case is *Boumar v. Belgium* (1987), which establishes only that to detain a 16 year old in a remand prison without any educational facilities for a total of 119 days in a year is not justified by Article 5.1(d). The only surprise in that is that the Belgian Government thought it worth arguing that the subparagraph did justify the remand. It does seem that the subparagraph will cover residential schools, attendance at which involves an element of compulsion, but the extent to which it will do so is undecided.

The second leg, which permits detention in order to bring a minor before the competent legal authority, is generally understood as equivalent to Article 5.1(c), though it does not state the elements relating to reasonable suspicion of having committed a criminal offence.

Mental illness and vagrancy

Article 5.1(e) permits the detention of five groups of persons:

* those whom it is necessary to detain in order to prevent the spread of infections diseases;
* persons of unsound mind;
* alcoholics;
* drug addicts; and
* vagrants.

The only cases to have gone before the Court have related to persons of unsound mind and to vagrants.

In *Winterwerp v. Netherlands* (1979–80) the Court held that the term "persons of unsound mind" cannot be given a definitive interpretation. It said, however, that the term cannot refer simply to someone whose views or behaviour deviate from the norms prevailing in a particular society because that would not be reconcilable with Article 5.1, whose object and purpose is to ensure that no-one is dispossessed of his liberty in an arbitrary fashion and which sets out an exhaustive list of exceptions calling for a narrow interpretation. The Court approved the practice of the Netherlands courts whereby the confinement of a "mentally ill person" was authorised only if his mental disorder was of such a kind or such a gravity as to make him an actual danger to himself or others. In *Ashingdane v. United Kingdom* (1985), the Court explained that one can derive from its case law three minimum conditions which have to be satisfied in order for there to be "the lawful detention of a person of unsound mind" within the meaning of Article 5.1(e):

- except in emergency cases, a true mental disorder must be established before a competent authority on the basis of objective medical expertise;
- the mental disorder must be of a kind or degree warranting compulsory confinement; and
- the validity of continued confinement depends upon the persistence of such a disorder.

In *Winterwerp*, the Court was prepared to accept that an emergency admission to hospital might extend for six weeks whilst the condition of the person concerned was being assessed, though there are indications in the judgement that the Court thought that six weeks was about the limit for that process. Also in *Ashingdane*, the Court said that held that the detention of persons of unsound mind must be in a suitable institution such as a hospital or clinic.

The meaning of the term "vagrant" was considered in two cases. In *Guzzardi v. Italy* (1980) it was held that it is not wide enough to include Mafia suspects without identifiable sources of income; but in *De Wilde* it was held that persons with no fixed abode, no means of subsistence and no regular trade or profession were within the concept of vagrant.

Immigration and extradition

Article 5.1(f) deals with the need for detentions in connection with immigration and extradition. As the Court recognised in *Chahal v. United Kingdom* (1996), States have the right, as a matter of well-established international law and subject to their treaty obligations including the Convention, to control the entry, residence and expulsion of aliens. The Court also noted in that case that the right to political asylum is not contained in either the Convention or its Protocols.

Article 5.1(f) authorises lawful arrest or detention for three purposes:

- to prevent unlawful entry to the country;
- deportation; and
- extradition.

The lawfulness criterion proved to be particularly important in *Bozano v. France* (1986). In that case, the applicant had been the subject of an extradition request to France from Italy following his conviction in absence in the Italian courts of abduction, attempted extortion, murder and various offences of indecency. The French Court refused extradition on the ground that trial in absence for serious offences without any requirement to hold a retrial in the presence of the accused was incompatible with French public policy. He was released from French custody. About a month later, in Limoges, where he lived, three plain clothes policemen forced him into an unmarked car. He was taken to Police Headquarters and served with a deportation order which required him to leave France. He was told that it was out of the question that he should be brought before the Appeals Board charged with dealing with such cases and was instead placed in a car and taken, not to the Spanish border (which was the closest) but to the Swiss border, 12 hours and several hundred kilometres away. From Switzerland he was extradited to Italy and there incarcerated to serve the life sentence which had been imposed on him in his absence. It is perhaps not surprising that the Court held that, viewing the circumstances as a whole, the applicant's deprivation of liberty was neither lawful nor compatible with the right to security of person.

MINIMUM RIGHTS FOR DETAINED PERSONS

Article 5.1 is concerned with the legitimacy of depriving a person of his or her liberty. The remainder of Article 5 provides for certain minimum rights for a person who is in that position.

Information about the reason for detention

Article 5.2 requires that such a person should be informed "promptly" (which means as soon as possible unless the person is in such a condition that he cannot understand what he is being told—*Clinton v. United Kingdom* (1995)) in a language which he understands (fluency is not necessary) of the reasons for his arrest and of any charge against him. In *Fox, Campbell and Hartley* (1990) it was held that the Article 5.2 guarantee means that the detained person must be told in simple, non technical language that he can understand the essential legal and factual grounds for his arrest so as to be able, if he sees fit, to challenge its lawfulness under Article 5.4. This formula suggests that a high degree of legal precision is not required; and, indeed, it has been held in that case and others that if the process of questioning itself makes the charge clear, Article 5.2 will be satisfied. Perhaps the most extreme example was *Dikme v. Turkey* (2000). In that case, the Court held that when a police officer said to a suspect: "You belong to *Devrimci Sol* [a left wing terrorist group] and if you don't give us the information we need the only way for you to get out of here will be as a corpse!" these words were sufficient to satisfy the requirements of Article 5.2. The Court considered that this most reprehensible statement gave a fairly precise indication of the nature of the suspicions entertained about the applicant. Having regard to that, to the fact that the organisation mentioned was illegal and to the reasons which might have prompted the applicant to hide his identity and to fear the police, the Court considered that the applicant should or could have realised at that stage that he was suspected of being involved in prohibited activities such as those of *Dev-Sol*, so that there had been no violation of Article 5.2.

Trial within a reasonable time or release pending trial

Article 5(3) entitles the accused to trial within a reasonable time or to release pending trial. It is clear that, in Convention terms, if the accused is to be kept in custody there must be relevant and sufficient grounds for doing so; but in *Tomasi v. France* (1993) it was held that suspicion alone was not enough to justify a remand in custody which lasted over five years. No exhaustive list of other reasons justifying the remand of the accused in custody exists. The principle was stated by the Court in *Letellier v. France* (1992) to be that the court before which the accused is brought must consider "all the facts arguing for and against the existence of a genuine requirement of public interest" for the remanding of the accused in custody. In *CC v. United Kingdom* (1999) the Commission said that:

> "the judge must examine all the facts arguing for and against the existence of a genuine requirement of public interest justifying, with due regard to the presumption of innocence, a departure from the rule of respect for the accused's liberty".

It is possible to classify the Strasbourg cases in four categories:

- prevention of crime;
- danger of flight;
- risk of interference with the course of justice; and
- prevention of public disorder.

This categorisation is, of course, no more than an analytical tool. As to the prevention of crime, it was held in *Toth v. Austria* (1992) that previous convictions could be relied on as giving reasonable grounds to fear that further offences would be committed. The danger of flight will vary according to the strength of the accused's ties with the jurisdiction and the court should consider financial guarantees (which include, but are not limited to, money bail) as a means of offsetting the risk (*Letellier; Matznetter v. Austria* (1979–80). The risk of interference with the course of justice requires to be kept under review and, if it disappears, liberation should follow unless there are other grounds for keeping the accused in custody (*Kemmache No. 1 v. France* (1992)) Finally, the cases on prevention of public disorder have related to terrorist offences (*Tomasi* (1993)) or the exceptional circumstances of a high profile, premeditated murder (*Letellier* (1992)).

Judicial determination of the lawfulness of detention

Article 5.4 provides that a person who has been deprived of his liberty must be able to take proceedings whereby the lawfulness of his detention is decided speedily by a court. This is a different issue from the *appropriateness* of a remand in custody, which is dealt with under Article 5.3. Under Article 5.4 it is the *lawfulness* of the detention which is in issue. In *Lamy v. Belgium* (1989) it was held that the principle of equality of arms applies to Article 5.4 so that the accused must be afforded the opportunity to present his case under conditions which do not place him at a substantial disadvantage *vis-à-vis* the prosecution.

COMPENSATION

Finally, Article 5.5 requires that everyone who has been the victim of arrest or detention in contravention of Article 5 shall have an enforceable right to compensation. That right is in the national courts and is not the same as the power of the Court to award just satisfaction (*Brogan* (1989); *Fox, Campbell and Hartley* (1990)).

It is important to understand that the right to compensation does not necessarily follow from a decision taken by an appeal court that a person should be released. It has to be established that the detention was not merely inappropriate but that it was in breach of Article 5. In *Perks and Others v. United Kingdom* (1999), each applicant had failed to pay sums due in respect of community charge (poll tax). At the time, the applicants were dependent on State benefits or living on a low income. In separate proceedings in magistrates' courts it was established that the non-payment was due to the debtor's wilful refusal or culpable neglect. Each of the applicants was thereupon committed to a term of imprisonment and detained. Legal aid was not available and the applicants were not legally represented before the magistrates' courts. The applicants were released on bail after applying for judicial review before the High Court. Following judicial review proceedings, each applicant obtained an order quashing the magistrates' imprisonment order in his or her case. The Court attached importance to the reasoning of the High Court judgments in the applicants' cases. In all of them, a key ground for the decision to quash was that the magistrates had not considered the alternative ways in which to exercise the discretion vested in them. In particular, they had failed to consider alternatives to imprisonment. But the High Court left open the possibility that the imprisonment orders were within the magistrates' jurisdiction, their defect being only a fettered exercise of discretion. It could not therefore be excluded that these orders were "flawed" or "unlawful" in the sense of being an unreasonable exercise of discretion but nevertheless fell within the jurisdiction of the courts by which they were made. The Court, therefore, did not find it established that the imprisonment orders were invalid, and thus unlawful.

---

6. RIGHT TO A FAIR HEARING (ARTICLE 6)

INTRODUCTION

Article 6 is in these terms:
> "1. In the determination of his civil rights and obligations or of any criminal charge against him, everyone is entitled to a fair and public hearing within a reasonable time by an independent and

impartial tribunal established by law. Judgment shall be pronounced publicly but the press and public may be excluded from all or part of the trial in the interests of morals, public order or national security in a democratic society, where the interests of juveniles or the protection of the private life of the parties so require, or to the extent strictly necessary in the opinion of the court in special circumstances where publicity would prejudice the interests of justice.

2. Everyone charged with a criminal offence shall be presumed innocent until proved guilty according to law.

3. Everyone charged with a criminal offence has the following minimum rights:

  a. to be informed promptly, in a language which he understands and in detail, of the nature and cause of the accusation against him;

  b. to have adequate time and facilities for the preparation of his defence;

  c. to defend himself in person or through legal assistance of his own choosing or, if he has not sufficient means to pay for legal assistance, to be given it free when the interests of justice so require;

  d. to examine or have examined witnesses against him and to obtain the attendance and examination of witnesses on his behalf under the same conditions as witnesses against him;

  e. to have the free assistance of an interpreter if he cannot understand or speak the language used in court."

Article 6 has accounted for far more of the case law of the Court than any other single Article. Indeed, if we leave aside Articles 5 and 8, we could probably say that Article 6 has generated more case law than all of the other Articles put together. Much of it relates to criminal law.

THE APPLICATION OF ARTICLE 6

It should be noted, first, that Article 6 applies to the *determination* of civil rights and obligations and of criminal charges. Several cases concerning civil rights and obligations have emphasised that Article 6 does not apply to proceedings which do not determine civil rights or criminal charges (*e.g. Brady v. United Kingdom* (1980) and *Koek v. Germany* (1987)). There have been fewer cases on the point arising out of criminal matters but it appears that Article 6 does not apply to those parts of proceedings which do not bear upon the determination of the charge. In particular, it does not apply to proceedings relating to deprivation of liberty which do not bear on the ultimate determination of the charge because they are dealt with by Article 5. In *X. v. Federal Republic of Germany* (1974) the applicant was a man charged with murder who complained that he had not been permitted to attend appeal proceedings relating to his remand in custody. The Commission held that, since the question of the determination of *the charge* did not arise, Article 6 did not apply.

Article 6 does not apply to investigations under the Companies Acts, even though they have a quasi-judicial character (*Fayed v. United Kingdom* (1994)). Nor does it apply to prison disciplinary proceedings even though they are in many ways analogous to criminal proceedings (*McFeeley v. United Kingdom* (1980)).

The Court pointed out in *Weeks v. United Kingdom* (1988) that matters of sentencing in general lie outside the scope of the Convention, but did hold in *T v. United Kingdom* (2000) that Article 6 applies to the sentencing phase and that that phase is not complete until the sentence has been definitively set. This means that, *inter alia*, the sentence must be fixed by an "independent and impartial tribunal established by law". That expression was held not to describe a Home Secretary.

More generally, in principle, one might expect that it would be possible to argue that a sentence of imprisonment is an interference with the right to respect for private and family life, so as to engage Article 8. In that event, it would be necessary for the authorities to satisfy the Article 8.2 necessity test, with emphasis no doubt falling on the question of proportionality. It is thought, however, that the disproportion would have to be quite extreme before a challenge on this basis could succeed. It should be borne in mind that in some cases the Court has been prepared to accept that deportation is proportionate in cases of serious crime (*Boughanemi v. France* (1996); *Bouchelkia v. France* (1997)).

The over-riding fairness requirement

Article 6.1 contains an over-riding requirement that the hearing should be "fair" and a number of specific requirements. Compliance with the specific rights set out in Article 6 will not alone guarantee that there has been a fair trial. The Court always looks at this question in the context of the trial as a whole. The concept of the "trial as a whole" includes any appeal proceedings (*Edwards v. United Kingdom* (1992); *Crociani, Palmiotti, Tanassi and Lefebre D'Ovidio v. Italy* (1981)) and even where there has been unfairness in the trial itself, the Court has been prepared to hold that such unfairness has been cured by what has happened on appeal (*Edwards*). The focus of the Court may therefore be said to be on the overall process of *determination* of the criminal charge rather than on the set-piece hearing itself.

By the same token, the focus is on the *process*. The case law of the Court does not comment on what the *outcome* of the trial should have been and even where it finds that there has been unfairness in the trial proceedings it refrains, sometimes explicitly, from saying that the accused should have been acquitted (*Saunders* (1996)). From this emphasis on fair process is derived the principle of equality of arms, by which a party is entitled to present his case under conditions which do not place him at a significant disadvantage *vis-à-vis* his opponent (*Dombo-Deheer BV v. Netherlands* (1994)).

The emphasis placed by the Court on over-riding fairness may be illustrated from *Asch v. Austria* (1993), in which the Court held that there was no breach even where, on the face of it, there was a *lack* of compliance with one of the specific guarantees construed narrowly but there was fairness over the procedure as a whole. In that case, the applicant's co-habitee had complained that he had assaulted her and there was medical evidence to show that she had sustained injuries consistent with that allegation. However, she subsequently returned to the police station to say that she and the applicant had been reconciled and that she had returned to live with him. She expressed her wish to withdraw her complaint. Despite this, the prosecutor proceeded with the case. The co-habitee refused to give evidence and her statement was read out by a police officer. The applicant was convicted.

The Court held that the guarantees in paragraph 3 of Article 6 are specific aspects of the right to a fair trial. Although the co-habitee had refused to testify at the hearing she should, for the purposes of Article 6.3(d), be regarded as a witness—a term to be given an autonomous interpretation—because her statements, as taken down in writing by a police officer and then related orally by him at the hearing, were in fact before the court, which took account of them. The Court considered that the admissibility of evidence is primarily a matter for regulation by national law and, as a rule, it is for the national courts to assess the evidence before them. The Court's task is to ascertain whether the proceedings considered as a whole, including the way in which evidence was taken, were fair. The Court said that all the evidence must normally be produced in the presence of the accused at a public hearing with a view to adversarial argument but that this does not mean that the statement of a witness must always be made in court and in public if it is to be admitted in evidence; in particular, this may prove impossible in certain cases. The use in this way of statements obtained at the pre-trial stage is not in itself inconsistent with paragraphs 3(d) and 1 of Article 6, provided that the rights of the defence have been respected. As a rule, these rights require that the defendant be given an adequate and proper opportunity to challenge and question a witness against him, either when he was making his statements or at a later stage of the proceedings.

The Court thought that it would clearly have been preferable if it had been possible to hear the co-habitee in person, but the right on which she relied in order to avoid giving evidence could not be allowed to block the prosecution, the appropriateness of which it was not for the Court to determine. Subject to the rights of the defence being respected, it was therefore open to the national court to have regard to the statement, in particular in view of the fact that it could consider it to be corroborated by other evidence before it, including the two medical certificates attesting to the injuries.

Furthermore, the Court said, the applicant had the opportunity to discuss the co-habitee's version of events and to put his own, first to the police and later to the court. However, on each occasion he gave a different version, which tended to undermine his credibility. It was clear from the file that the co-habitee's statements did not constitute the only item of evidence on which the first instance court based its decision. It also had regard to the personal assessment made by the police officer as a result of his interviews with the co-habitee and the applicant, to the two concurring medical certificates, to the police investigation and to the other evidence appearing in the applicant's file. The fact that it was impossible to question the co-habitee at the hearing did not therefore, in the circumstances of the case, violate the rights of the defence and did not deprive the accused of a fair trial. Accordingly, there had been no breach of paragraphs 1 and 3(d) of Article 6, taken together.

At first, this result appears startling to British eyes. Article 6.3(d) reads like a guarantee of the right to cross examine and that plainly was not afforded to the applicant. The approach of the Court, however, was to emphasise overall fairness and, finding no unfairness in what had happened, to find no breach of Article 6.

It is also important to note that the Court said, in *Doorson v. The Netherlands* (1996):

> "It is true that Article 6 does not explicitly require the interests of witnesses in general, and of those of victims called upon to testify in particular, to be taken into consideration. However, their life, liberty or security of person may be at stake, as may interests coming generally within the ambit of Article 8 of the Convention. Such interests of witnesses and victims are in principle protected by other, substantive provisions of the Convention, which imply that Contracting States should organise their criminal proceedings in such a way that those interests are not unjustifiably imperilled. Against this background, principles of fair trial also require that in appropriate cases the interests of the defence are balanced against those of witnesses and victims called upon to testify."

This may be seen in the context of the Court's earlier remark in *Soering v. United Kingdom* (1989), that:

> "inherent in the whole of the Convention is a search for a fair balance between the demands of the general interest of the community and the requirements of the protection of the individual's fundamental rights" (a remark made in the context of Article 3 ECHR, which might well be the most absolute of the Convention rights).

The High Court of Justiciary has, in *Montgomery and Coulter v. H.M. Advocate* (1999) noted the importance of over-riding fairness. In that case, the Lord Justice-General said that:

> "the only right which Article 6.1 protects is the right to a fair trial and so, in considering a case founded upon that Article, the Court is concerned only with whether the appellants will receive a fair trial...The appellants' rights under the Human Rights Convention exist not to punish the Crown for what may or may not have been unwise decisions, but to ensure that any trial which the appellants

face is fair. In this respect, the protection afforded to accused persons under the Convention is similar to the protection afforded by the plea of oppression".

Notice should be taken of *X. v. Austria* (1963) in which it was said that a virulent press campaign against the accused might violate the right to fair trial, though the case law recognises that much may depend on the way in which the trial judge deals with possible prejudice in directing the jury (*X. v. United Kingdom* (1978)).

The same principle, of fairness over the trial as a whole, arose in *Teixeira de Castro v. Portugal* (1998). In that case, police officers hoped that through a drug addict and small time dealer they would be able to identify a more significant drug supplier. Unaware that they were police officers, the man agreed to find a supplier and mentioned the name of the applicant. A meeting eventually took place, at which the officers said that they wished to buy drugs. The applicant agreed to procure heroin and, through intermediaries, did so. The police officers then identified themselves and arrested the applicant, who was in due course convicted and sentenced him to six years' imprisonment. He complained of a breach of Article 6.

The Court analysed the matter primarily in terms of overall fairness rather than on the detained wording of any part of Article 6. It held that the use of undercover agents must be restricted and safeguards put in place even in cases concerning the fight against drug trafficking and that the public interest cannot justify the use of evidence obtained as a result of police incitement. On the facts of the particular case, the Court concluded that the two police officers' actions went beyond those of undercover agents because they instigated the offence and there was nothing to suggest that without their intervention it would have been committed. That intervention and its use in the impugned criminal proceedings meant that, from the outset, the applicant was deprived of a fair trial so that there had been a violation of Article 6.1.

THE RIGHT TO A COURT

The first specific identifiable right in Article 6.1 is the right to a hearing, sometimes called the "right to a court". We have already seen, from *Golder v. United Kingdom*, that the Court rejected a Government argument that Article 6 regulates the conduct of the hearing but does not create a right to a hearing as such. Nevertheless, the right is not unlimited. There is a right to a hearing in the determination of

- civil rights and obligations
- criminal charges.

These concepts are autonomous and whether or not something is a matter of civil right or obligation or a criminal charge according to national law is of limited significance.

A number of cases before the Court and the Commission have made it clear that these categories are not unlimited but it is very difficult to extract principles of general applicability from the cases. The Court examines the particular circumstances of each dispute and comes to a conclusion after something of a balancing exercise taking into account all of the competing factors.

Civil rights and obligations

It can be said that matters within the category of private law, such as the law of tort or delict, family law or the law of property, will always constitute civil rights and obligations (see, for example, *Axen v. Federal Republic of Germany* (1983), *Airey v. Ireland* (1979-80), *Buchholz v. Federal Republic of Germany* (1980) and *Langborger v. Sweden* (1989)). The relationship between the individual and the State, dealt with under the heading of public law, is likely to be a matter of civil right or obligation if the right in question is a pecuniary one (*Editions Périscope v. France* (1992); *Stran Greek Refineries and Stratis Andreadis v. Greece* (1994)). In *Schouten and Meldrum v. The Netherlands* (1995) the Court said that there may exist "pecuniary" obligations *vis-à-vis* the State or its subordinate authorities which, for the purpose of Article 6.1, are to be considered as belonging exclusively to the realm of public law and are accordingly not covered by the notion of "civil rights and obligations". The Court said that, apart from fines imposed by way of "criminal sanction", this will be the case, in particular, where an obligation which is pecuniary in nature derives from tax legislation or is otherwise part of normal civic duties in a democratic society. In that case, the Court then went on to conduct a detailed balancing exercise on whether Dutch social security contributions had more in common with tax or with insurance premiums. It concluded that insurance premiums were a closer analogy, so that Article 6 did apply; but that conclusion depended on the particular nature of the Dutch scheme. *Application against Finland* (1995) is an example of a case which went in the other direction with the Commission holding that a dispute about a refusal to issue a passport was not within the scope of Article 6.

Criminal charge

The concept of the criminal charge is somewhat less complex. In *Engel*, the Court noted in relation to military offences that all the Contracting States make a distinction of long standing, albeit in different forms and degrees, between disciplinary proceedings and criminal proceedings. For the individuals affected, the former usually offer substantial advantages in comparison with the latter, for example as concerns the sentences passed. Disciplinary sentences, in general less severe, do not appear in the person's criminal record and entail more limited consequences. The Court said that, in order to determine whether there is a criminal charge, for the purposes of Article 6, it is necessary to know as a starting point whether the provision(s) defining the offence charged belong, according to the legal system of the respondent State, to criminal law, disciplinary law or both concurrently. The indications so afforded have only a formal and relative value and have then to be examined in the light of the common denominator of the respective legislation of the various Contracting States. Then, the Court explained, the nature of the offence is a factor of greater import. When a service-man finds himself accused of an act or omission allegedly contravening a legal rule governing the operation of the armed forces, the State may in principle employ against him disciplinary law rather than criminal law. But where the aim is the imposition of serious punishments involving deprivation of liberty the "charges" will come within the "criminal" sphere and Article 6 will be applicable.

These rules were applied in *Östürk v. Federal Republic of Germany* (1984). The applicant had been dealt with in respect of a minor road traffic accident in which he was at fault and had been required to pay a rather modest administrative penalty of DM60. The German Government argued that Article 6 did not apply to this procedure. However, the Court noted that, according to the ordinary meaning of the terms, there generally come within the ambit of the criminal law offences that make their perpetrator liable to penalties intended, *inter alia*, to be deterrent and usually consisting of fines and of measures depriving the person of his liberty. In addition, misconduct of the kind committed by Mr. Östürk continued to be classified as part of the criminal law in the vast majority of the Contracting States, as it had been in the Federal Republic of Germany until the entry into force of the decriminalising legislation. Moreover, the changes related essentially to procedural matters and to the range of sanctions, which retained a punitive character, which is the customary distinguishing feature of criminal penalties. The rule of law infringed by the applicant had undergone no change of content. It was a rule that was directed, not towards a given group possessing a special status — in the manner, for example, of disciplinary law — but towards all citizens in their capacity as road-users. The Court considered that the general character of the rule and the purpose of the penalty, being both deterrent and punitive, sufficed to show that the offence in question was, in terms of Article 6 of the Convention, criminal in nature.

The Court added that there is nothing to suggest that the criminal offence referred to in the Convention necessarily implies a certain degree of seriousness and that it would be contrary to the object and purpose of Article 6, which guarantees to "everyone charged with a criminal offence" the right to a court and to a fair trial, if the State were allowed to remove from the scope of this Article a whole category of offences merely on the ground of regarding them as petty.

PUBLIC HEARING

In the cases to which it applies, Article 6 requires that the hearing should be in public. In *Axen*, the Court said that the purpose of the guarantee of a public hearing is to protect litigants "against the administration of justice in secret with no public scrutiny; it is also one of the means whereby confidence in the courts, superior and inferior, can be maintained. By rendering the administration of justice visible, publicity contributes to the achievement of the aim of Article 6.1, namely a fair trial". The Article goes on, however, to authorise the exclusion of the public and even of the press:

"in the interest of morals, public order or national security in a democratic society, where the interests of juveniles or the protection of the private life of the parties so require, or to the extent strictly necessary in the opinion of the court in special circumstances where publicity would prejudice the interests of justice."

This part of Article 6 has not been the subject of much consideration by the Strasbourg organs. There was comment in *Campbell and Fell v. United Kingdom* (1985) that ordinary criminal proceedings nearly always take place in public, notwithstanding security problems; but this passage was descriptive and not normative. Moreover, the reference was made simply to draw a distinction between an ordinary trial and prison disciplinary proceedings (with which that case was concerned). In *X. v. Austria* (1965) the Commission approved the exclusion of the public from a trial for sexual offences against children, without identifying the reasoning which led to that conclusion; so the case scarcely goes beyond what is said in the plain words of the Convention. In *Monnell and Morris v. United Kingdom* (1987) the Court held that a decision to grant or refuse of leave to appeal, the question being whether the appellant has demonstrated the existence of arguable grounds, was of such a limited nature as not to call for oral argument at a public hearing or the personal appearance of the prospective appellant. In *Martin v. United Kingdom* (1999) the Court applied *Monnell and Morris* and held that an application which attacked the sifting of appeals by the High Court of Justiciary was manifestly ill founded.

HEARING WITHIN A REASONABLE TIME

Article 6.1 requires that the hearing should proceed "within a reasonable time". The purpose of this was said, in *Stögmüller v. Austria* (1979–80) to be to protect against excessive procedural delays. In criminal cases, the period to be taken into consideration commences when the accused has been charged, which means, for Convention purposes, the date when official notification is given to him by a competent authority that it is alleged that he has committed an offence, or the date from which his situation is substantially affected as a result of the suspicion against him (*Eckle v. Germany* (1983)). In some cases, this will be the date of arrest (*Wemhoff v. Germany* (1979–80)) but since the accused is not always arrested, in some cases another means of identifying the relevant stage must be sought. It is likely that the police, by cautioning and charging the accused, will start the clock running. It might be argued that the date on which the police first interview the accused as a suspect should be the date from which time is counted but this seems to go too far. In *Neumeister v. Austria* (1979–80) the applicant appeared for the first time as a suspect before an Investigating Judge on January 21, 1960. On that date he was interrogated and released. He was arrested and placed in detention on February 23, 1961 and the Court treated that as the date on which he had been charged. In *H.M. Advocate v. McLean* (1999), the High Court of Justiciary rejected the proposition that actions by the Social Work Department and Reporter to the Childrens' Panel, taken without reference to the police or procurator fiscal, could start the clock.

The period to be taken into account lasts until the determination of the charge and that includes any appeal (*Neumeister*; *Monnell and Morris*). Neither the Convention nor the Court has set out any absolute period of time within which proceedings must be completed if the requirement for trial within a reasonable time is to be met. Reasonableness will, the Court has said, always be a matter of particular circumstances (*König v. Germany* (1980)). It seems clear too that, whilst the High Court of Justiciary is alert to the risk that concentrating on domestic standards would lead to Article 6.1 being applied differently in different countries (with the perverse result that a breach is more likely to be found in countries with legal systems that are generally efficient), judges of the High Court will consider the circumstances of each case in light of their general knowledge of the Scottish criminal justice system. The Lord Justice General said as much in *H.M. Advocate v. McGlinchey and Renicks* (2000). In that case, the High Court took the view that a timescale of just over three years was not unreasonable even though that period included approximately six months of inactivity while the trial judge delayed in providing a report for appeal purposes. The Lord Justice-General observed that many cases in the Scottish criminal justice system take just as long, though for different reasons.

Trial within a reasonable time is the Convention rights issue which has most clearly altered the law since the entry into force of section 57(2) of the Scotland Act 1998. The development of the law began with *Little v. H.M. Advocate* (1999), in which the first-instance judge considered in particular what was said in *Eckle (*1983) and took the view that it is not necessary for the person who is subject to the charge to demonstrate that the delay has resulted in prejudice. The correctness of that analysis was confirmed by the Justiciary Appeal Court in *McNab v. H.M. Advocate* (1999). That court said that it is important to note:

"...there is a clear distinction between a plea based on oppression in the ordinary sense and a plea based on a right under Article 6.1. The former is concerned with the question whether, by reason of delay or some other cause, the prospects of the accused receiving a fair trial have been gravely prejudiced ... The latter, on the other hand, is concerned with the alleged failure to bring a case to trial within a reasonable time. It follows that, in order to demonstrate that it is incompatible with his or her right for the prosecutor to insist on the trial, the accused does not require to show that prejudice has been or is likely to be suffered thereby."

The Court further noted, however, that:

"as a matter of common sense and ordinary experience it is unrealistic to expect that all cases should progress towards trial at the same speed. Each makes its own particular demands in regard to preparation. Some cases are subject to the imperative created by the fact that the accused is remanded in custody. Others have features which call for special expedition. Pressure of business may lead to proceedings taking longer than they would otherwise have done. In the end of the day the question whether more than "a reasonable time" had elapsed depends on our assessment of the various factors to which we have referred, against the background of our general knowledge as to the criminal justice system in Scotland."

The approach taken by both the European Court and the High Court of Justiciary is to look first at the delay and then, if the time taken appears prima facie unreasonable, to require the State or the Crown (as the case may be) to explain the delay. In the case law of the Court, it is possible to identify three factors as important, these being:

- the complexity of the case ;
- the conduct of the applicant; and
- the conduct of the authorities.

These factors are taken cumulatively. The Court makes its own assessment of the reasonableness of the time in a given case (there is no margin of appreciation) but it does so having regard to the fact that Article 6 can only require such expedition as is consistent with the proper administration of justice (*Stögmüller*). It has recognised as relevant to the criterion of complexity:

- the volume of evidence (Eckle);
- the number of accused persons or charges (*Neumeister*);
- the need to obtain expert evidence (*Wemhoff*);
- the need to obtain evidence from abroad (*Neumeister*); and
- the complexity of the legal issues involved (Neumeister).

These categories are not closed.

It needs to be stressed, moreover, that the entitlement to a hearing within a reasonable time is not confined to criminal cases. *Caillot v. France* (1999) and *Nunes Violante v. Portugal* (1999) both concerned the Article 6.1 right to a hearing within a reasonable time in the determination of civil rights. In February 1990 the applicant in *Caillot* sought from the *Tribunal Administratif* of Caen an annulment of a decision of the commission charged with responsibility for land consolidations, which he regarded as being to his disadvantage. The proceedings were only concluded in May 1996, with a decision of the *Conseil d'Etat*—a delay of six years and three months. Three years and 4 months of that were attributable to the procedure in the *Conseil d'Etat*. The Government argued that this delay was not significant enough to amount to a breach of the Convention. *Nunes Violante* concerned a claim from a union pension fund in respect of a work injury. It had already lasted over 9 years and was still not resolved when the case was heard in Strasbourg. The Portuguese Government argued that this period did not constitute unreasonable delay but the Judgment of the Court does not explain on what basis the Government maintained that position.

In both cases, the Court reiterated that whether or not a delay is reasonable will depend on the complexity of the issue, the conduct of the applicant and the conduct of the authorities. The cases in question were not complex and there were significant periods of inactivity. In *Caillot*, the Court said that it is incumbent on States to organise their judicial systems so as to guarantee to everyone the right to obtain a decision within a reasonable time. It did not consider that the time which elapsed while the case was in the *Conseil d'Etat* could be regarded as reasonable and awarded the applicant 25,000FF in just satisfaction. Nor did it regard the delay in *Nunes Violante* as reasonable and it awarded 800,000PTE with expenses.

The response of both France and Portugal in these cases seems to have consisted of little but an assertion that the period in question was not unreasonable. Whilst every case must be considered on its own facts, it seems clear from *Eckle* that there comes a time when a delay becomes prima facie inordinate and it then falls to the respondent state to come forward with explanations. In a civil cause it seems unlikely that the consequence of a delay will be to prevent the pursuer or plaintiff proceeding with some or all of his case (as in *Little*). Apart from any other consideration, that would be likely to bring about a breach of his own Convention right to an effective remedy before national courts in respect of breaches of other Convention rights (though since Article 13 is not incorporated that matter would have to be pursued in Strasbourg). It might, however, be that parties would have a remedy against the Court Service in respect of the delay.

INDEPENDENT AND IMPARTIAL TRIBUNAL

The next element particularly specified by Article 6.1 is that the tribunal which determines the charge should be independent and impartial and established by law.

Security of tenure
The first aspect of this is that the judge should have reasonable security of tenure, so as to protect him or her against undue influence. As the Commission put it in *Zand* v. *Austria* (1978):

> "...according to the principles of the rule of law in democratic states which is the common heritage of the European countries, the irremovability of judges during their term of office, whether it be for a limited period of time or for lifetime, is a necessary corollary of their independence from the Administration and thus included in the guarantees of Article 6.1 of the Convention."

The particular judge

The other aspect of the guarantee relates to the particular judge in the case; and here we begin by considering *Pullar v. United Kingdom* (1996) in which the applicant complained that he had not had a fair trial because one of jurors was employed by a prosecution witness.

The Court held that the view taken by the accused with regard to the impartiality of the tribunal could not be conclusive. What mattered was whether his doubts could be held to be objectively justified. Although the principle of impartiality is an important element in support of the confidence which the courts must inspire in a democratic society, the Court said that:

> "it does not necessarily follow from the fact that a member of a tribunal has some personal knowledge of one of the witnesses in a case that he will be prejudiced in favour of that person's testimony. In each individual case it must be decided whether the familiarity in question is of such a nature and degree as to indicate a lack of impartiality on the part of the tribunal."

The Court took note of the fact that the employee was only one of 15 jurors, that the jury was directed to dispassionately assess the credibility of all the witnesses before them and that all of the jurors took an oath to similar effect. It held that there was no breach of Article 6.1. A somewhat similar approach was taken in *Hauschildt v. Denmark* (1989).

Pullar concerned the jury but contains material which is helpful in considering the position of the judge. The Court said in *Pullar* that:

> "the principal that a tribunal shall be presumed to be free of prejudice or partiality is long established in the case-law of the court."

This presumption is extremely strong and in fact, in the European jurisprudence, no claim of bias by a judge seems ever to have been successful. In *Piersack v. Belgium* (1982), however, the Court did comment that a judge in respect of whom there was a legitimate reason to fear partiality must withdraw.

ARTICLE 6.2

The presumption of innocence

The classic statement of the primary meaning of Article 6.2 is to be found in *Barberà, Messegué and Jabardo v. Spain* (1989):

> "Paragraph 2 embodies the principle of the presumption of innocence. It requires, *inter alia*, that when carrying out their duties the members of a court should not start with the preconceived idea that the accused has committed the offence charged, and any doubt should benefit the accused."

Presumptions

The Court has also addressed presumptions under the heading of Article 6.2. In *Salabiaku v. France* (1991) it said that:

"presumptions of fact or of law operate in every legal system. Clearly the Convention does not prohibit such presumptions in principle. It does, however, require the Contracting States to remain within certain limits in this respect as regards criminal law...It requires States to confine them within reasonable limits which take into account the importance of what is at stake and maintain the rights of the defence".

The critical issue is whether there is a facility for rebutting the presumption in question.

The right to silence

The Court has derived a right to silence from the presumption of innocence stipulated by Article 6.2 but it held in *Murray v. United Kingdom* (1996) that the right is not absolute. In that case the evidence against the applicant had been formidable. The Court said that:

"on the one hand it is self evident that it is incompatible with the immunities under consideration to base a conviction solely or mainly on the accused's silence or on a refusal to answer questions or to give evidence himself. On the other hand, the Court deems it equally obvious that these immunities cannot and should not prevent that the accused's silence, in situations which clearly call for an explanation from him, be taken into account in assessing the persuasiveness of evidence adduced by the prosecution".

This was further considered in *Condron v. United Kingdom* (2000). The applicants had stood trial in 1995 on charges of supplying heroin and possession of heroin with intent to supply. The prosecution case relied, among other things, on the fact that a police surveillance team had observed the applicants passing various items to their neighbour and co-accused from the balcony of their flat. At the time of their interview with the police, the applicants' solicitor considered that they were not fit to be questioned since they were suffering from heroin withdrawal symptoms; the doctor who examined them at the police station disagreed with their solicitor's assessment. Before the start of their interview the applicants were cautioned. During the interview the applicants remained silent and did not reply to questions concerning the above-mentioned items. The applicants gave evidence at their trial and offered an explanation as to why certain items were seen to be exchanged over their balcony. The applicants also declared that they had not answered police questions because their solicitor had advised that they were not in a fit condition to be interviewed. With reference to section 34 of the Criminal Justice and Public Order Act 1994, the trial judge gave the jury the option of drawing an adverse inference from the applicants' silence during interview. The applicants were found guilty. Although the Court of Appeal found the trial judge's direction to the jury on the question of the applicants' silence deficient, it was satisfied that the convictions were safe.

The Court observed that whether the drawing of inferences from an accused's silence during police interview infringed Article 6 was a matter to be determined in the light of all the circumstances of the case. The fact that the question of an accused's silence was left to the jury could not, of itself, be considered incompatible with Article 6. However, given that the right to silence lay at the heart of the notion of a fair procedure guaranteed by that Article, the Court stressed, in line with its *Murray* judgment, that particular caution was required before a domestic court could invoke an accused's silence against him. It reiterated in this connection that it would be incompatible with the right to silence to base a conviction solely or mainly on the accused's silence or on a refusal to answer questions or to give evidence himself. This being said, it was obvious that the right cannot and should not prevent that the accused's silence, in situations which clearly call for an explanation from him, be taken into account in assessing the persuasiveness of the evidence adduced by the prosecution.

The Court noted that the applicants put forward an explanation at their trial for their failure to mention during the police interview why certain items were exchanged between them and their co-accused. They testified that they remained silent on their solicitor's advice. Although the trial judge drew the jury's attention to the applicants' explanation for their silence, the Court considered that he did so in terms which left the jury at liberty to draw an adverse inference notwithstanding that it may have been satisfied as to the plausibility of the explanation. In the Court's opinion, as a matter of fairness, the jury should have been directed that if it was satisfied that the applicants' silence at the police interview could not sensibly be attributed to their having no answer or none that would stand up to cross-examination it should not draw an adverse inference.

The Court noted that the responsibility for deciding whether or not to draw an inference rested with the jury and it was impossible to ascertain what weight, if any, was given to the applicants' silence since a jury did not provide reasons for its decisions. The Court concluded that the applicants were denied a fair hearing, in violation of Article 6.1.

Different considerations apply to compulsory powers to require answers to questions. In *Saunders v. United Kingdom* (1996) a breach of Article 6.2 was found where the prosecution made extensive use at trial of answers obtained from the accused under compulsory powers in sections 432 and 442 of the Companies Act 1985.

It should be noted that, in *Saunders*, the Court pointed out that, as commonly understood in the legal systems of the Contracting Parties to the Convention and elsewhere, the right to silence does not extend to the use in criminal proceedings of material which may be obtained from the accused through the use of compulsory powers but which has an existence independent of the will of the suspect such as, inter alia, documents acquired pursuant to a warrant, breath, blood and urine samples and bodily tissue for the purpose of DNA testing.

ARTICLE 6.3

Article 6.3 gives everyone charged with a criminal offence certain minimum rights.

Information about the charge
Article 6.3(a) has on its face the following elements:

- the accused must be informed of the nature and cause of the accusation;
- that information must be given promptly;
- that information must be detailed;
- that information must be given in a language which the accused understands.

It is worth noting that, in *Bricmont v. Belgium* (1986) the Commission said that the general purpose of this is to give the accused person the information he needs to prepare his defence.

In *Gea Catalan v. Spain* (1995) the Court approved of the Commission's interpretation of Article 6.3(a). What the Commission said was that:

> "the accused is entitled to be informed not only of the cause of the accusation, *i.e.* the material facts alleged against him which form the basis of the accusation, but also of the nature of the accusation, *i.e.* the legal classification of those material facts".

The circumstances in that case were that the applicant had taken advantage of his position as an employee of the Bank of Fomento to cause the bank to discount in his favour a number of bills of exchange which he had himself drawn, using false names. He was charged with obtaining property by deception as provided for in the Spanish Criminal Code. In pre-trial submissions the public prosecutor referred to a statutory aggravation of the offence but as a result of a typing error the reference given was to Article 529(1) of the Criminal Code; it should have been to Article 529(7). The applicant complained that he had not been informed of a component of the charge against him. The Court, however, held that the discrepancy complained of was clearly the result of a mere clerical error. It could not see how the applicant could complain that he had not been informed of all of the components of the charge since the prosecution case must have been obvious from its pre-trial submissions and since it should have been obvious that the aggravation provided for in Article 529(1) had no application to the facts alleged but that Article 529(7) did. It therefore held that there was no breach.

Next, the accused is entitled to be given the information "promptly". In *Application against Italy* (1988) the Commission held that the principal underlying purpose of the requirement for promptness, by which compliance will be judged, is to afford the accused time for the preparation of his defence.

In *Broziek v. Italy* (1990), the Court was satisfied with an indictment which specified date and place, listed the offences charged, referred to the relevant Article of the Criminal Code and identified the victim.

Language is addressed by Article 6.3(a) and translation by Article 6.3(e). *Kamasinski v. Austria* (1991) is relevant to both subparagraphs. In that case, the Court, whilst holding that the inadequacy of translation in the particular case did not in fact result in an unfair trial, did express clear views on the question of the translation of documents, including the indictment. So far as the general right to interpretation of documents is concerned, what they said was as follows:

"The right, stated in paragraph 3(e) of Article 6, to the free assistance of an interpreter applies not only to oral statements made at the trial hearing but also to documentary material and the pre-trial proceedings. Paragraph 3(e) signifies that a person 'charged with a criminal offence' who cannot understand or speak the language used in court has the right to the free assistance of an interpreter for the translation or interpretation of all those documents or statements in the proceedings instituted against him which it is necessary for him to understand or to have rendered into the court's language in order to have the benefit of a fair trial. However, paragraph 3(e) does not go so far as to require a written translation of all items of written evidence or official documents in the procedure. The interpretative assistance provided should be such as to enable the defendant to understand the case against him and to defend himself, notably by being able to put before the court his version of events".

As regards the indictment in particular, the Court said that, whilst Article 6.3(a):

"does not specify that the relevant information should be given in writing or translated in written form for a foreign defendant, it does point to the need for special attention to be paid to the notification of the 'accusation' to the defendant. An indictment plays a crucial role in the criminal process, in that it is from the moment of its service that the defendant is formally put on written notice of the factual and legal basis of the charges against him. A defendant not conversant with the court's language may in fact be put at a disadvantage if he is not also provided with a written translation of the indictment in a language he understands".

The Court did not hold, and has not held, that the provision of a written translation of the indictment will always be necessary to the fairness of the trial. In the *Kamasinski* case itself, the Court held that there was no unfairness despite the lack of such a translation. In so holding, they were influenced by a number of factors:

- the indictment was not complex;
- the applicant had been questioned at length by the police and investigating judges and must have been aware of the accusations levelled against him;

- notwithstanding the absence of a translation, the applicant had challenged the indictment on the ground of insufficiency of evidence;
- at no time did the applicant request that the indictment be translated;
- when asked at the start of the trial, the applicant had told the trial court that he understood the charges.

Preparation for trial

Article 6.3(b) entitles the accused to adequate time and facilities for the preparation of his defence. In *Edwards* (1992), the Court said that it is a requirement of fairness that the prosecution authorities disclose to the defence all material evidence for or against the accused. That followed *Jespers v. Belgium* (1982) in which the Commission said that:

"in any criminal proceedings brought by a state authority, the prosecution has at its disposal, to back the accusation, facilities deriving from its powers of investigation, supported by judicial and police machinery with considerable technical resources and means of coercion. It is in order to establish equality, as far as possible, between the prosecution and the defence that national legislation in most countries entrusts the preliminary investigation to a member of the judiciary or, if it entrusts the investigation to the Public Prosecutor's Department, instructs the latter to gather evidence in favour of the accused as well as evidence against him."

The Commission further took the view that the facilities to be provided should:

"include the opportunity to acquaint himself, for the purposes of preparing his defence, with the results of investigation carried out throughout the proceedings...In short, Article 6, paragraph 3(b) recognises the right of the accused to have at his disposal, for the purposes of exonerating himself or of obtaining a reduction in his sentence, all relevant elements that have been or could be collected by the competent authorities. The Commission considers that, if the element in question is a document, access to that document is a necessary "facility"...if, as in the present case, it concerns acts of which the defendant is accused, the credibility of testimony, etc."

The Court said in *Kremzow v. Austria* (1994) that restriction of the right to inspect the court file to an accused's lawyer is not incompatible with the rights of the defence under Article 6.

Defence in person or through legal assistance

Article 6.3(c) entitles the accused to defend himself in person or through legal assistance of his own choosing. Trial in absence was said in *Poitrimol v. France* (1994) not to be incompatible with the Convention in principle if the person concerned can subsequently obtain from a court which has heard him a fresh determination of the merits of the charge, in respect of both law and fact. The Court went on to say that it is open to question whether this latter requirement applies when the accused has waived his right to appear and to defend himself, but that at all events such a waiver must, if it is to be effective for Convention purposes, be established in an unequivocal manner and be attended by minimum safeguards commensurate with its importance.

As to legal assistance of his own choosing, in *Croissant v. Germany* (1993), the accused person had appointed lawyers whose places of business were geographically remote from the trial court, with the result that adjournments were likely. In order to avoid that, the trial court appointed a further defence lawyer who practised in the same city as the court. The accused person complained of a breach of Article 6.3(c) but the Court found against him. It said that:

"notwithstanding the importance of a relationship of confidence between lawyer and client, this right cannot be considered to be absolute. It is necessarily subject to certain limitations where legal aid is concerned and also where, as in the present case, it is for the courts to decide whether the interests of justice require that the accused be defended by counsel appointed by them. When appointing defence counsel the national courts must certainly have regard to the defendant's wishes...However, they can over-ride those wishes when there are relevant and sufficient grounds for holding that this is necessary in the interests of justice."

Examining witnesses

Article 6.3(d) provides, so far as relevant, that the accused is entitled to "have examined the witnesses against him". The U.K. lawyer would read that and tend to take the view that hearsay is absolutely excluded. Support for that position would be derived from a superficial reading of *Unterpertinger v. Austria* (1991), in which the applicant had been accused of assault upon his wife and step-daughter. They had made statements to the police but declined to give evidence. He was convicted on the basis of the statements given to the police. The Court delivered a short judgement. The starting point was that:

"the reading out of statements in this way cannot be regarded as being inconsistent with Article 6.1 and 3(d) of the Convention, but the use made of them as evidence must nevertheless comply with the rights of the defence, which it is the object and purpose of Article 6 to protect. This is especially so where the person 'charged with a criminal offence', who has the right under Article 6.3(d) to 'examine or have examined' witnesses against him, has not had an opportunity at any stage in the earlier proceedings to question the persons whose statements are read out at the hearing."

The conviction had been based "mainly" on the statements made by the wife and step-daughter, which the Austrian court had treated as proof of the truth of the accusations rather than merely as what the Court referred to as "information". In these circumstances, it was held, the applicant's defence rights had been "appreciably restricted" so that he had not had a fair trial. The Court held that there had been a breach of

Article 6.1 taken with "the principles inherent in paragraph 3(d)"; but it is significant that the Court said that the reading out of statements was not in itself inconsistent with the Convention.

The Court went further in *Asch* (1993) holding that there had been no breach where the conviction was based in part upon the statement given to the police by the complainer in the case, who was the applicant's co-habitee and who had refused to give evidence at trial. However, it was of importance in that case that the evidence of the co-habitee was not the only evidence in the case. The police had observed injuries to the complainer and there was, in addition, medical evidence (though it does not seem to have addressed the identity of the assailant). It was also of importance that the applicant, when interviewed, had given several conflicting accounts of how the complainer came by her injuries which, the Court said, "tended to undermine his credibility".

Interpreters

For material on Article 6.3(e), see the consideration of *Kamasinski* at page 55 above.

---

7. PROHIBITION OF RETROSPECTIVE CRIMINALISATION (ARTICLE 7)

INTRODUCTION

Article 7 is concerned exclusively with criminal law. It provides:

"1. No one shall be held guilty of any criminal offence on account of any act or omission which did not constitute a criminal offence under national or international law at the time when it was committed. Nor shall a heavier penalty be imposed than the one that was applicable at the time the criminal offence was committed.

2. This article shall not prejudice the trial and punishment of any person for any act or omission which, at the time when it was committed, was criminal according to the general principles of law recognised by civilised nations."

In *Kokkinakis v. Greece* (1994), the Court said that Article 7.1:

"embodies...the principle that only the law can define a crime and prescribe a penalty (*nullum crimen, nulla poena sine lege*) and the principle that the criminal law must not be extensively construed to an accused's detriment, for instance, by analogy; it follows from this that an offence must be clearly defined in law. This condition is satisfied where the individual can know from the wording of the relevant provision and, if need be, with the assistance of the court's interpretation of it, what acts and omissions will make him liable."

COMMON LAW AND ARTICLE 7

The Commission has treated common law offences as unobjectionable in themselves but has made a distinction between that which clarifies the law and that which extends it such that it is made to "cover facts which previously clearly did not constitute a criminal offence" (*X Ltd and Y Ltd v. United Kingdom* (1982)). As regards clarification, the Commission has said in the same case that "it is not objectionable that the existing elements of the offence are clarified and adapted to new circumstances which can reasonable be brought under the original conception of the offence".

In *SW and CR v. United Kingdom* (1996), the Court recalled the words used in *Kokkinakis* and said that from those principles it followed that an offence must be clearly defined in the law. This requirement is satisfied where the individual can know from the wording of the relevant provision and, if need be, with the assistance of the courts' interpretation of it, what acts and omissions will make him criminally liable. The Court thus indicated that when speaking of "law" Article 7 alludes to the same concept as that to which the Convention refers elsewhere when using that term, a concept which comprises written as well as unwritten law and implies qualitative requirements, notably those of accessibility and foreseeability.

The Court pointed out that, however clearly drafted a legal provision may be, in any system of law, including criminal law, there is an inevitable element of judicial interpretation. There will always be a need for elucidation of doubtful points and for adaptation to changing circumstances. Indeed, in the United Kingdom, as in the other Convention States, the progressive development of the criminal law through judicial law-making is a well entrenched and necessary part of legal tradition. Article 7 of the Convention cannot be read as outlawing the gradual clarification of the rules of criminal liability through judicial interpretation from case to case, provided that the resultant development is consistent with the essence of the offence and could reasonably be foreseen. The Court considered that it could reasonably be foreseen that there would be judicial recognition of the absence of immunity on the part of a husband and commented too that the essentially debasing character of rape is so manifest that the result could not be said to be at variance with the object and purpose of Article 7 of the Convention, namely to ensure that no one should be subjected to arbitrary prosecution, conviction or punishment. What was more, the abandonment of the unacceptable idea of a husband being immune against prosecution for rape of his wife was in conformity not only with a civilised concept of marriage but also, and above all, with the fundamental objectives of the Convention, the very essence of which is respect for human dignity and human freedom.

PENALTY

The issue of the imposition of a heavier penalty than that available at the time of the offence was considered in *Welch v. United Kingdom* (1995). The applicant was arrested and charged in November 1986 in relation to drug trafficking offences. In January 1987 the Drug Trafficking Offences Act 1986 came into force, making it possible for the first time for English courts to impose confiscation orders. In February and May 1987 the applicant was charged with further drug trafficking offences. In August 1988 he was convicted of five counts. He was imprisoned and a confiscation order was imposed in the sum of £66,914 (subsequently reduced on appeal to £59,914). He complained under Article 7 that the imposition of a confiscation order constituted a retroactive criminal penalty. The Government argued that the true purpose of a confiscation order was two-fold: firstly, to deprive a person of the profits which he had received from drug trafficking and secondly, to remove the value of the proceeds from future use in the drugs trade. On this basis, the Government argued, confiscation was not a penalty. The Court, held, however, that the concept of a penalty in Article 7 is an autonomous Convention concept. The wording of Article 7.1 indicates that the starting point for the assessment of the existence of a penalty is whether the measure is imposed following conviction for a criminal offence. Other factors that may be taken into account are the nature and purpose of the measure in question, its characterisation under national law, the procedures involved in the making and implementation of the measure and its severity. These factors are, of course, familiar from consideration of the term "criminal charge" in relation to Article 6.

The Court noted that, before a confiscation order can be made in English law, the accused must have been convicted of a drug trafficking offence. This link is not diminished by the fact that, due to the operation of the statutory presumptions concerning the extent to which the accused has benefited from drug trafficking, the court order may affect proceeds which are not directly related to the facts underlying the criminal conviction. The 1986 Act was introduced to overcome the inadequacy of existing powers of forfeiture. Although the provisions were designed to ensure that proceeds were not available for use in future drug trafficking and that crime does not pay, the legislation also pursues the aim of punishing the offender. The aims of prevention and reparation are consistent with a punitive purpose and may be seen as constituent elements of the very notion of punishment.

Several aspects of the making of an order under the 1986 Act were in keeping with the idea of a penalty even though they were essential to the preventive scheme inherent in the 1986 Act. These included the sweeping statutory assumptions that all property passing through the offender's hands during a six-year period is the fruit of drug trafficking unless he can prove otherwise, the fact that the confiscation order is directed to proceeds and not restricted to actual enrichment or profit, the discretion of the trial judge in fixing the order to take account of the degree of culpability of the accused and the possibility of imprisonment in default of payment. These elements, considered together, provided a strong indication of *inter alia* a regime of punishment. Looking behind appearances at the reality of the situation, whatever the characterisation of the measure of confiscation, the fact remained that the applicant faced more far reaching detriment as a result of the order than that to which he was exposed at the time of the commission of the offences of which he was convicted. There was therefore a breach of Article 7; but the Court stressed that its conclusion related only to the retrospective application of the legislation and did not call into question in any respect the powers of confiscation conferred on the courts as a weapon in the fight against the scourge of drug trafficking.

INTERNATIONAL LAW AND GENERAL PRINCIPLES OF LAW

The references in paragraph 2 to offences under international law and to things which are criminal according to the general principles of law recognised by civilised nations have not been considered by the Court. However, in terms of international law, very few offences are within these categories. Piracy, slavery, genocide and the waging of a war of aggression are certainly within the categories and torture probably is (*R. v. Bow Street Metropolitan Stipendiary Magistrate and others, ex p. Pinochet Ugarte (No. 3)* (1999)).

---

8. RIGHT TO RESPECT FOR PRIVATE LIFE (ARTICLE 8)

INTRODUCTION

Article 8 provides:
> "1. Everyone has the right to respect for his private and family life, his home and his correspondence.
> 2. There shall be no interference by a public authority with the exercise of this right except such as is in accordance with the law and is necessary in a democratic society in the interests of national security, public safety or the economic well-being of the country, for the prevention of disorder or crime, for the protection of health or morals, or for the protection of the rights and freedoms of others."

This has been one of the most dynamically interpreted provisions of ECHR and it has an extremely wide application. We have seen, in *Johnstone v. United Kingdom*, that Article 8 has relevance to family law.

We shall see in a moment that its scope is far wider than merely that. First, however, we deal with the structure of Article 8, which follows a pattern common to many of the Convention rights in that it states a right and then states the circumstances in which interference with the right may be permitted.

THE STRUCTURE OF ARTICLE 8

Paragraph 1 and the opening words of paragraph 2 state the right: in this case, the right to respect for private and family life, home and correspondence and the prohibition on interference with the right. Paragraph 2 then effectively qualifies this, stating the circumstances in which interference with the right may be permitted. In *Funke v. France* (1993), the Court said that the exceptions provided for by Article 8.2 are to be interpreted narrowly. Under Article 8.2, before interference with the right is permitted it must, first, be in accordance with the law. Secondly, it must be necessary. Thirdly, it must be in pursuit of one of the specified objectives.

On reading the cases, it becomes very clear that the Court analyses Article 8 issues within a well established framework which consists of five questions:

- Is the right relevant to what has happened?
- Is there an interference with the right?
- Is the interference in accordance with law?
- Does the interference pursue one of the permitted objectives?
- Is the interference necessary? This question has two parts. First, the Court asks if there was a "pressing social need" for the interference. Secondly, it asks whether what was done was proportionate to the need.

THE INTERESTS PROTECTED

The first question, then, is whether the right is relevant at all. It will be seen that there are four areas which are protected (though they will sometimes overlap). They are:

- private life;
- family life;
- home;
- correspondence.

The core meanings of these phrases are clear enough; but they have all, to a greater or lesser extent, attracted extended meanings.

Private life
In *X and Y v. The Netherlands* (1985) the Court said that the concept of the private life covers the physical and moral integrity of the person, including his or her sexual life (which was the aspect at issue in that case). Within that sphere, if the applicant had a reasonable expectation

of privacy, he or she will be successful in establishing that Article 8 is relevant.

Whether such an expectation existed and was reasonable will, of course, be questions to be assessed on the facts of the individual case. In *Halford v. United Kingdom* (1997) the applicant was held to have had a reasonable expectation of privacy for telephone calls from her office, especially because one of her office phones was specifically designated for her private use and because she had been given an assurance that she could use her office telephones for the purposes of the sex-discrimination case which she was pursuing against her employers (a police force). By contrast, in *Friedl v. Austria* (1995) it was held that a person taking part in a demonstration in a public place has no reasonable expectation of privacy (the complaint was that the police had taken the applicant's photograph). Again, whilst the Court was entirely satisfied that persons of homosexual orientation serving in the British armed forces had a reasonable expectation of privacy as regards their sexual practices (*Lustig-Prean and Beckett and Smith and Grady v. United Kingdom* (2000)) it regarded it as seriously open to question whether the same could be said of a group of up to 44 men who engaged in sado-masochistic practices (involving the inflicting of injuries) with each other, video recording the proceedings and distributing those recordings within the group (*Laskey, Jaggard and Brown v. U.K.* (1997)).

Family

In *Keegan v. Ireland* (1994), the Court held that the notion of the "family" in Article 8 is not confined solely to marriage-based relationships and may encompass other *de facto* "family" ties where the parties are living together outside of marriage. A child born out of such a relationship is part of that "family" unit from the moment of his birth and by the very fact of it. There thus exists between the child and his parents a bond amounting to family life even if at the time of his or her birth the parents are no longer co-habiting or if their relationship has then ended.

Home

"Home" is not a concept which is limited to the place where the applicant is actually living at any given time. In *Gillow v. United Kingdom* (1986), the applicants owned a house on Guernsey to which they always intended to return and kept their furniture in it. Since the first applicant's work required them to live elsewhere, they let the house to tenants over a period of almost 19 years. When they moved back to the house, the first applicant was prosecuted for breach of housing legislation which restricted the categories of persons entitled to live on the island. The Court held that, although the applicants had not lived in the house for 19 years, they had in fact retained sufficient continuing links with it for it to be considered their "home", for the purposes of Article 8.

"Home" need not even be a house. In *Niemietz v. Germany* (1992), which concerned the search by the police of a lawyer's office, the Court noted that in certain Contracting States the concept of the "home" had been accepted as extending to business premises and that such an interpretation was fully consonant with the French text, since the word "domicile" has a broader connotation than the word "home" and may extend, for example, to a professional person's office. More generally, the Court considered, to interpret the words "private life" and "home" as including certain professional or business activities or premises would be consonant with the essential object and purpose of Article 8, namely to protect the individual against arbitrary interference by the public authorities.

Correspondence

Correspondence plainly covers letters. In *Campbell v. United Kingdom* (1992) there was a breach of Article 8 where prison authorities opened and read letters between a prisoner and, amongst others, the European Commission on Human Rights. But it also covers telephone calls (*Halford*; *Malone v. United Kingdom* (1984)) and there does not seem to be any reason why it should not extend to other methods of communication, such as e-mail.

INTERFERENCE

Given that one of the interests protected by Article 8 is relevant, the next question is whether there is an interference with the right. In many cases, the answer will be obvious. Tapping telephones will amount to an interference (*Halford*; *Malone*); so will searching a house or office (*Funke*; *Niemitz*). In *Keegan* the secret placing of a child for adoption, so severing any possible link with the father (who was separated from the mother) was an interference. It would be possible to multiply endless examples. What is less obvious, however, is the fact that it is enough if a state of affairs exists which puts an applicant's Article 8 interests at risk. In *Norris v. Ireland* (1991) the applicant was an active homosexual and a campaigner for homosexual rights. He objected in particular to the existence in Ireland of laws which made certain homosexual practices between consenting adult men criminal offences. Although prosecutions had been confined in practice to cases involving minors, there was no bar to prosecution in the case of such consenting adults. The Court held that, since there was a possibility of prosecution, the maintenance in force of the legislation constituted a continuing interference with the applicant's right to respect for his private life.

JUSTIFICATION FOR INTERFERENCE

Introduction

If it is established that Article 8 is relevant to whatever has happened and that there has been an interference with the right which it guarantees, there will be a breach of the Article unless the respondent State establishes that the criteria set out in paragraph 2 are met.

Accordance with law

The first criterion is that the interference was in accordance with law. In *Malone* the Court explained that the phrase "in accordance with the law" does not merely refer back to domestic law but also relates to the quality of the law, requiring it to be compatible with the rule of law, which is expressly mentioned in the preamble to the Convention. The phrase thus implies that there must be a measure of legal protection in domestic law against arbitrary interferences by public authorities with the rights safeguarded by paragraph 1. The position was made still clearer in *Khan v. United Kingdom* (2000). In that case, police officers investigating an allegation of drug trafficking against certain persons including the applicant had installed a listening device in a house occupied by one of those persons. The installation was not in accordance with any rule of law but neither was it prohibited by any rule of law. Tape recorded conversations obtained by using that listening device constituted the totality of the prosecution case against the applicant. He objected to the admissibility of the evidence of the tape recordings but the trial judge declined to exclude the evidence under section 78 of the Police and Criminal Evidence Act 1984 and the applicant thereafter pled guilty, whereupon he was sentenced to a period of imprisonment.

Before the Court it was conceded by the U.K. Government that the use of a covert listening device in this way amounted to an interference with the right to respect for private life guaranteed by Article 8.1 of the Convention. Rejecting the U.K.'s submission that the existence of Home Office Guidelines to govern surveillance of this sort, constituted the necessary "law" for the purposes of Article 8.2, the Court noted that, since such guidelines were neither legally binding nor directly publicly accessible, there was no domestic law regulating the use of covert listening devices at the relevant time and held that the interference could not, therefore, be considered to be "in accordance with law" as required by Article 8.2. There was, therefore, a breach of Article 8 and it was not necessary for the court to go further and consider whether the interference was necessary and pursued one of the specified legitimate aims.

Legitimate aim

Assuming that the State establishes that whatever was done was in accordance with law, the next question will be whether it pursued one of the specified legitimate aims. It will be recalled that the Court said in *Funke* (1993) that these aims are exhaustive and to be construed narrowly.

Necessary

Although the question of necessity appears in paragraph 2 before that of legitimate aim, it is frequently considered last by the Court. That is because it is often the most complex and finely balanced question in any Article 8 case.

In *Dudgeon v. United Kingdom* (1981) it was explained that "necessary" in the context of Article 8 does not have the flexibility of such expressions as "useful", "reasonable", or "desirable", but implies the existence of a "pressing social need" for the interference in question. The Court said that it is for the national authorities to make the initial assessment of the pressing social need in each case and accordingly, a margin of appreciation is left to them.

In *Lustig-Prean and Beckett v. United Kingdom* (2000) the State overstepped the mark. The applicants had both served in the Royal Navy but had been dismissed on account of their homosexuality. Prior to the discovery of their sexual orientation, both had received highly complimentary reports on their performance. When it came to the attention of the Naval authorities that they might be homosexual, investigations were commenced and both applicants were interviewed. At those interviews they both acknowledged their homosexuality but the interviews continued and the second applicant in particular was asked highly detailed questions about his sexual practices. The applicants complained that the investigations into their homosexuality and their subsequent discharge from the Royal Navy on the sole ground that they were homosexual, in pursuance of the Ministry of Defence's absolute policy against homosexuals in the British armed forces, constituted a violation of their right to respect for their private lives protected by Article 8 of the Convention.

The Court reiterated that an interference would be considered "necessary in a democratic society" for a legitimate aim if it answered a pressing social need and, in particular, was proportionate to the legitimate aim pursued. Given the matters at issue in the present case, the Court underlined the link between the notion of "necessity" and that of a "democratic society", the hallmarks of the latter including pluralism, tolerance and broadmindedness. The Court said that when the relevant restrictions concern a most intimate part of an individual's private life, there must exist particularly serious reasons before such interferences can satisfy the requirements of Article 8.2 of the Convention. The core argument of the Government in support of the policy of dismissal was that the presence of open or suspected homosexuals in the armed forces would have a substantial and negative effect on morale and, consequently, on the fighting power and operational effectiveness of the armed forces. The Court found, however, that the perceived problems were founded solely upon the negative attitudes of heterosexual personnel towards those of homosexual orientation. The Court noted the lack of concrete evidence to substantiate the alleged damage to morale and fighting power that any change in the policy would entail. The Court considered it reasonable to assume that some difficulties could be anticipated as a result of any change in policy but was of the view that it had not been shown that conduct codes and disciplinary rules could not adequately deal with any behavioural issues arising. Accordingly, the Court concluded that convincing and weighty reasons had not been offered by the Government to justify the policy against homosexuals in the armed forces or, therefore, the consequent discharge of the applicants from those forces. In sum, the Court found that neither the investigations conducted into the applicants' sexual orientation, nor their discharge on the grounds of their homosexuality in pursuance of the Ministry of Defence policy, were justified under Article 8.2 of the Convention.

Proportionality

In *Lustig-Prean* the Court referred to the question of proportionality. That issue has been a consistent feature of the case law on Article 8 (and other Articles). What is meant is that, if an interference is to be regarded as necessary, it must be proportionate to the aim which it is sought to achieve. Lack of proportionality was the basis of the decision in *McLeod v. United Kingdom* (1999). In that case, in connection with divorce proceedings, the applicant was ordered by a County Court to deliver to her ex-husband a number of items and furniture from the former matrimonial home, where she lived with her elderly mother. The ex-husband arrived at the former matrimonial home, accompanied by his brother and sister and a solicitor's clerk. Fearing that there would be a breach of the peace because of Mrs McLeod's previous unwillingness to comply with orders of the court, her ex-husband's solicitors had arranged for two police officers to be present while the property was being removed. Mrs McLeod was not at home when her ex-husband and his party arrived. Her mother allowed them to enter the house and remove property. When the applicant returned home, she objected to the removal of the property. One of the police officers intervened and insisted that she allow her former husband to leave with the property. The Court considered that the police could not be faulted for responding to the solicitors' request for assistance, since there had been a genuine fear that a breach of the peace might occur when Mr McLeod removed his property from the former matrimonial home but considered that as soon as it became apparent that Mrs McLeod was not at home, the officers should not have entered the house, since it should have been clear to them that there was little or no risk of disorder or crime occurring. On these grounds, the Court found that the officers' entry had been disproportionate to the legitimate aim pursued and that there had been a violation of Article 8 of the Convention.

POSITIVE OBLIGATIONS

We have seen in Chapter 1 that some of the Articles of the Convention carry with them positive obligations. That was illustrated in Chapter 1 by reference to *López Ostra* and it arose also in *Johnston v. Ireland*. Further examples are to be found in *Marckx v. Belgium* (1979-80) and *X and Y v. The Netherlands* (1985).

In *Marckx*, the applicants were a journalist and her illegitimate daughter. Under Belgian law, no legal bond between an unmarried mother and her child resulted from the mere fact of birth. Whilst the birth certificate recorded at the register office sufficed to prove the maternal affiliation of a married woman's children, the maternal affiliation of an illegitimate child required further procedure before it was established. The establishment of maternal affiliation had certain consequences for the extent of the child's family relationships and consequent rights of access and maintenance, and for her inheritance rights. To place the child on the same footing as a legitimate child, the mother had to adopt her. The Court held that by proclaiming the right to respect for family life, Article 8 imposes a positive obligation on the State to act in a manner calculated to allow those concerned to lead a normal family life. Respect for family life implies in particular the existence in domestic law of legal safeguards that render possible, from the moment of birth, the child's integration in its family-which the particular legal regime applicable in the case failed to do.

In *X and Y v. the Netherlands*, the second applicant was mentally handicapped and had been living since 1970 in a privately-run home for mentally handicapped children. On the night after her 16th birthday a relative of a member of staff forced the girl to follow him to his room, to undress and to have sexual intercourse with him. The incident had traumatic consequences for her, causing her major mental disturbance. When he found out what had happened, her father (the first applicant) went to the local police station to file a complaint and to ask for criminal proceedings to be instituted. Rape could not be proved but there was an offence which applied to a person who "through gifts or promises ... through abuse of a dominant position resulting from factual circumstances, or through deceit, deliberately causes a minor of blameless conduct to commit indecent acts with him or to suffer such acts from him", but in case of that kind, the offender could be prosecuted only on complaint by the actual victim. The victim, being mentally handicapped, was unable to make such a complaint and there could therefore be no prosecution.

The Court recalled that although the object of Article 8 is essentially that of protecting the individual against arbitrary interference by the public authorities, it does not merely compel the State to abstain from such interference: in addition to this primarily negative undertaking, there may be positive obligations inherent in an effective respect for private or family life. These obligations, it said, may involve the adoption of measures designed to secure respect for private life even in the sphere of the relations of individuals between themselves. The choice of the means calculated to secure compliance with Article 8 in the sphere of the relations of individuals between themselves is in principle a matter that falls within the Contracting States' margin of appreciation. In this connection, there are different ways of ensuring "respect for private life", and the nature of the State's obligation will depend on the particular aspect of private life that is at issue. Recourse to the criminal law is not necessarily the only answer. However, the protection afforded by the civil law in the case of wrongdoing of the kind inflicted on the second applicant was insufficient. This was a case where fundamental values and essential aspects of private life were at stake. Effective deterrence was indispensable in this area and it could be achieved only by criminal-law provisions. Since the law did not provide the second applicant with practical and effective protection, it had to be concluded, taking account of the nature of the wrongdoing in question, that she was the victim of a violation of Article 8.

---

9. RIGHT TO RESPECT FOR FREEDOM OF THOUGHT, CONSCIENCE AND RELIGION (ARTICLE 9)

INTRODUCTION

The scheme of Article 9 is very similar to that of Article 8. Paragraph 1 states the right and paragraph 2 states the basis on which that right may be limited. The full text is as follows:

> "1. Everyone has the right to freedom of thought, conscience and religion; this right includes freedom to change his religion or belief and freedom, either alone or in community with others and in public or private, to manifest his religion or belief, in worship, teaching, practice and observance.
>
> 2. Freedom to manifest one's religion or beliefs shall be subject only to such limitations as are prescribed by law and are necessary in a democratic society in the interests of public safety, for the protection of public order, health or morals, or for the protection of the rights and freedoms of others."

It should be noted at the outset that the right belongs to individuals, not to companies, because a company lacks the capacity to have a conscience or religious belief (*Company X v. Switzerland* (1981)). It should also be noted that in *Manoussakis and Others v. Greece* (1997) the Court said that the right to freedom of religion as guaranteed under the Convention excludes any discretion on the part of the State to determine whether religious beliefs or the means used to express such beliefs are legitimate.

THOUGHT, CONSCIENCE AND RELIGION

There are three concepts involved in this right and they are not synonymous:

- thought;
- conscience; and
- religion

The extent to which thought, conscience and religion overlap has not really been explored in the case law. It is clear, both from the text and from *Kokkinakis v. Greece* (1993) (in which the Court said that as well as being vital for believers, the right is also a "precious asset for atheists, agnostics, sceptics and the unconcerned") that thought and conscience are not merely subheadings of religion. In the case law of the Commission and the Court (which is very limited) the main focus has, however, been on religion (because that has been the heading under which most applicants have gone to the Court).

"PRACTICE"

One exception to this is *Arrowsmith v. United Kingdom* (1978) in which the applicant argued that her distribution of pacifist leaflets to soldiers (in respect of which she was convicted) was motivated by her pacifist beliefs and hence protected by Article 9. The Commission accepted that pacifism falls within the ambit of the right to freedom of thought, conscience and religion but held that the term "practice" in Article 9.1 does not cover absolutely every act which is motivated or influenced by a religion or a belief. In *Larissis and Others v. Greece* (1998) the Court recalled this principle in holding that there had been no breach of Article 9 where members of the Pentecostal church had been convicted of proselytism (in some circumstances an offence under Greek law) where those whom they sought to convert were their subordinates in the Greek airforce and testified that they had felt under pressure because of the difference in rank. In the same case, however, the Court held that there was a breach in respect of convictions for attempting to convert civilians who did not feel themselves under any pressure. This approach applied a distinction drawn in *Kokkinakis*. In that case, the Court said that bearing Christian witness and improper proselytism are not the same thing. The former, it said, corresponds to true evangelism, which a report drawn up in 1956 under the auspices of the World Council of Churches described as an essential mission and a responsibility of every Christian and every Church. The latter, the Court said, represents a corruption or deformation of it. Improper proselytism, according to the WCC report, may take the form of activities offering material or social advantages with a view to gaining new members for a Church or exerting improper pressure on people in distress or in need; it may even entail the use of violence or brainwashing. These practices, the Court said, are not compatible with respect for the freedom of thought, conscience and religion of others.

The Commission applied a similar approach in cases in which applicants had attempted, on the basis of their religious beliefs, to withhold tax since that tax went into a general fund, some of which was used to purchase armaments. The Commission said (in *H; B v. United Kingdom* (1986)) that Article 9:

"primarily protects the sphere of personal beliefs and religious creeds, i.e. the area which is sometimes called the forum internum. In addition, it protects acts which are intimately linked to these attitudes, such as acts of worship or devotion which are aspects of the practice of a religion or belief in a generally recognised form. However, in protecting this personal sphere, Article 9 of the Convention does not always guarantee the right to behave in the public sphere in a way which is dictated by such a belief: for instance by refusing to pay certain taxes because part of the revenue so raised may be applied for military expenditure....The obligation to pay taxes is a general one which has no specific conscientious implications in itself".

ARTICLE 9 AS AN ALTERNATIVE TO OTHER ARTICLES

Some applicants have noted that paragraph 2 permits the State to interfere with the manifestation of religion or beliefs but that there is in the Convention no basis on which the State can interfere with freedom of thought or conscience. This has meant that Article 9 becomes an attractive alternative to other Articles, such as Article 8, which permit more wide ranging State interference. If an applicant can characterise an issue as relating to the realm of thought or conscience rather than simply to his or her private or family life (for example) the fact that the State might, in response to a pressing social need, have been acting lawfully and proportionately in pursuit of an Article 8.2 objective becomes irrelevant. The Court has, however, consistently declined to accept such lines of argument. In *Hoffman v. Austria* (1993) the applicant was unsuccessful in invoking Article 9 in relation to the custody of children where the parents had different religious beliefs; the Court dealt with the issue under Article 8. In *Young, James and Webster v. United Kingdom* (1981) issues relating to the refusal, out of conviction, of the applicants to join a trade union were addressed by the Court under Article 11, not Article 9.

10. RIGHT TO FREEDOM OF EXPRESSION (ARTICLE 10)

INTRODUCTION

Article 10 provides

"1. Everyone has the right to freedom of expression. This right shall include freedom to hold opinions and to receive and impart information and ideas without interference by public authority and regardless of frontiers. This Article shall not prevent States from requiring the licensing of broadcasting, television or cinema enterprises.

2. The exercise of these freedoms, since it carries with it duties and responsibilities, may be subject to such formalities, conditions, restrictions or penalties as are prescribed by law and are necessary in a democratic society, in the interests of national security, territorial integrity or public safety, for the prevention of disorder or crime, for the protection of health or morals, for the protection of the reputation or rights of others, for preventing the disclosure of information received in confidence, or for maintaining the authority and impartiality of the judiciary."

Like other Articles, Article 10 begins by stating the right and then goes on to state the qualifications and restrictions which apply to it. It will be seen that the structure of paragraph 2 bears a marked similarity to that of Article 8.2, in that it adopts the same formula of "prescribed by law", "necessary" and legitimate objectives. Many of the objectives are the same as those which apply to Article 8 but there are certain additional ones. There is also a preamble which explains that the exercise of the freedom carries with it duties and responsibilities. In *Bergens Tidende and Others v. Norway* (2000) the Court pointed out that by reason of the "duties and responsibilities" inherent in the exercise of freedom of expression, the safeguard afforded by Article 10 to journalists in relation to reporting on issues of general interest is subject to the proviso that they must act in good faith in order to provide accurate and reliable information in accordance with the ethics of journalism.

THE AMBIT OF THE RIGHT

The right to freedom of expression is a right which is guaranteed to all. It was made clear in *Casada Coca v. Spain* (1994) that "No distinction is made in it according to whether the type of aim is profit making or not". This principle enabled the applicant in that case to complain (albeit ultimately unsuccessfully) that it was a breach of Article 10 for him as a lawyer to be penalised for advertising.

Paragraph 1 makes it clear that the right includes freedom to hold opinions and to receive and impart information and ideas. In terms of the definition, it has a very wide ambit. Also in *Casada Coca*, the Court said that Article 10:

"does not apply solely to certain types of information or ideas or forms of expression, in particular those of a political nature; it also encompasses artistic expression, information of a commercial na-ture...and even light music and commercials transmitted by cable".

The Article has been held applicable not only to advertisements (*Casada Coca*) but also to investigative journalism (*Sunday Times v. United Kingdom* (1979–80)) and to artistic works. In *Muller v. Switzerland* (1988), the Court explained that Article 10 does not distinguish between the various forms of expression. Indeed, Article 10 applies even where the work in question might be regarded as devoid of any real artistic merit. In *Muller*, the Swiss appellate court rejected evidence that the paintings at issue had any artistic merit, observing that in them "sexual activity is crudely and vulgarly portrayed for its own sake and not as a consequence of any idea informing the work".

This is not to say that considerations of morality have no relevance to Article 10; merely that the proper approach is to address those considerations under the heading of Article 10.2, which sets out the cases in which there may be interference with the right to freedom of expression.

The concept of freedom of expression, then, is a wide one but it is not unlimited. The words "freedom of expression" have to be given their ordinary meaning in their context and that context deals with opinions, information and ideas. In *Stevens v. U.K.* (1986) the Com-mission held that it does not include expressing oneself sexually by having intercourse; the application in that case was by a serving prisoner who complained that being prevented from having sexual relations was a breach of Article 10. In *Kosiek v. F.R.G.* (1986) the applicants were unsuccessful in their attempt to bring the attachment of conditions to their employment as teachers within Article 10. On the facts, what the complaint was really about was rights of access to public employment.

INTERFERENCE WITH THE RIGHT

In the range of cases to which the right to freedom of expression does properly apply, the interferences with which the Court has typically had to deal have frequently involved interdicts or injunctions and convictions for obscenity and contempt of court. There is no doubt that all of these things are interferences. The Court explained in *Handyside v. United Kingdom* (1979–80) and *Sunday Times v. United Kingdom* (1979–80) that an interference entails a violation of Article 10 if it does not fall within one of the exceptions provided for in paragraph 2. Where this stage is reached, the Court therefore has to examine in turn whether the interference "prescribed by law", whether it had an aim or aims that is or are legitimate under Article 10.2 and whether it was "necessary in a democratic society" for that aim or aims.

PRESCRIBED BY LAW AND LEGITIMATE AIMS

The expression "prescribed by law" is by now a familiar one that does not require elaboration; though it is worth noting that in *Casado Coca* the Statute of the Spanish Bar was a sufficient basis for a finding that this criterion was satisfied. Similarly, the acceptable aims which paragraph 2 articulates are, for the most part, familiar. The key question under Article 10 has usually been whether the necessity of the interference has been made out.

NECESSITY

Politics

It is well recognised that States have a wide margin of appreciation in this matter but it has also to be recognised that this margin is appreciably narrowed where the purpose of the expression involved is political rather than commercial or artistic. In *Castells v. Spain* (1992) the applicant had been convicted of the offence of insulting the Government. He was an elected member of the Spanish legislature and he had published an article in which he alleged inactivity on the part of the authorities, in particular the police, in face of terrorist murders in the Basque country and even collusion between the police and the guilty parties. In convicting him, the national court stressed that the State could be threatened by attempts to discredit democratic institutions. In the context of a considerable terrorist campaign the Court was willing to accept that the proceedings instituted against the applicant were brought for the prevention of disorder within the meaning of Article 10.2.

The Court noted that the applicant had made his criticism in a periodical and pointed out that the "pre-eminent role of the press in a State governed by the rule of law" must not be forgotten. Although it must not overstep various bounds set for the prevention of disorder and the protection of the reputation of others, it is, the Court said, nevertheless incumbent on it to impart information and ideas on political questions and on other matters of public interest. Freedom of the press affords the public one of the best means of discovering and forming an opinion of the ideas and attitudes of their political leaders. The Court said that free political debate is at the very core of the concept of a democratic society, though it added that the freedom of political debate is not absolute in nature. In an important passage, it went on to say:

> "The limits of permissible criticism are wider with regard to the Government than in relation to a private citizen, or even a politician. In a democratic system the actions or omissions of the Government must be subject to the close scrutiny not only of the legislative and judicial authorities but also of the press and public

opinion. Furthermore, the dominant position which the Government occupies makes it necessary for it to display restraint in resorting to criminal proceedings, particularly where other means are available for replying to the unjustified attacks and criticisms of its adversaries or the media."

Similarly, the Court has taken an unsympathetic view to attempts to restrain political protest. In *Steel and others v. United Kingdom* (1999) the third, fourth and fifth applicants had been engaged in a peaceful protest outside the "Fighter Helicopter II" conference in London, a marketing event, at which combat helicopters were being sold. They were all arrested and presented to court from custody. On that occasion, the case was adjourned and, when it next called, the prosecution offered no evidence, so the case was dismissed. On their application to the Commission, the Court held that there had been a breach of Article 10. The applicants had been committing no offence and their arrest was, therefore, an interference with the exercise of their right to freedom of expression which was disproportionate to the prevention of disorder and protection of the rights of others as authorised by the Convention.

The Press
There is also a tendency on the part of the Court to be unsympathetic to attempts to restrain press freedom. There were elements of this in *Castells* but it appears still more clearly in cases which have been pursued in Strasbourg by newspapers or journalists themselves. The best known example of this is the *Sunday Times* case in which the Court held (by a narrow margin of 9–7) that an injunction obtained by the Attorney General restraining publication of an article was not necessary in that it did not meet a pressing social need. The context was that there was ongoing litigation about the drug "thalidomide" which had been taken by a number of pregnant women and which had caused deformities in their children. The article was part of a newspaper campaign to secure a better settlement for the claimants and was to address the history of the testing, manufacture and marketing of the drug. The injunction proceeded on the basis that the article would constitute a contempt of court.

The Court said Art.10 is of particular importance where the press is concerned and that whilst the mass media must not overstep the bounds imposed in the interests of the proper administration of justice, it is incumbent on them to impart information and ideas concerning matters that come before the courts. "Not only do the media have the task of imparting such information and ideas", said the Court, "the public also has a right to receive them". In the particular case, the families of the victims had a vital interest in knowing the underlying facts and they could be deprived of that information "only if it appeared absolutely certain that its diffusion would have presented a threat to the authority of the judiciary."

A similar determination to protect the freedom of the press appeared in *Barthold v. F.R.G.* (1985). In that case, a vet who had been campaigning for a round-the-clock veterinary emergency service, was party to a newspaper article which described how the life of a cat had been saved only because he provided such a service. This got him into difficulties with his professional body and resulted ultimately in him being the subject of an order restraining him from publishing certain types of material.

The Court found a breach of Article 10, noting that the article had pursued the specific object of informing the public about a situation at a time when the enactment of new legislation on veterinary surgeons was under consideration. The Court said that freedom of expression constitutes one of the essential foundations of a democratic society and one of the basic conditions for its progress and for the development of every man and woman. The necessity for restricting that freedom for one of the purposes listed in Article 10.2 must be convincingly established.

When considered from this viewpoint, the interference complained of went further than the requirements of the legitimate aim pursued. The domestic law presumed that a professional who wrote an article intended to act for the purposes of commercial competition as long as that intent has not been entirely over-ridden by other motives; but the Court considered that a criterion as strict as this in approaching the matter of advertising and publicity in the liberal professions is not consonant with freedom of expression. Its application risks discouraging members of the liberal professions from contributing to public debate on topics affecting the life of the community if ever there is the slightest likelihood of their utterances being treated as entailing, to some degree, an advertising effect. By the same token, application of a criterion such as this is liable to hamper the press in the performance of its task of purveyor of information and public watchdog.

By contrast, we should note *Ahmed and others v. United Kingdom* (2000), which concerned restrictions on the political activities of some relatively senior local government employees. The Court held that the interferences which resulted from the application of the restrictions to the applicants pursued the legitimate aim of protecting the rights of others, council members and the electorate alike, to effective political democracy at the local level. The intention behind the regulations was to underpin the long tradition of political neutrality which local government officers owed to elected council members and to ensure that the effectiveness of local political democracy was not diminished through the corrosion of the neutrality of certain categories of officers characterised by the sensitivity of their functions. The restrictions were in part a reaction to specific instances of abuse of power by certain local government officers and that there was increased potential for more widespread abuse in the light of the trend towards confrontational politics in local government affairs. The restrictions were a valid response to that problem and they only applied to carefully defined categories of senior officers distinguished by the nature of the activities which they performed and in respect of which political impartiality was

a paramount consideration. The right to join a political party was not
affected but only the freedom of senior officers to make public
pronouncements which appeared to be of a party political nature.

Other issues

States have been much more successful where the expression of political
views has not been the matter for consideration. In *Handyside* (1979-80)
the Court held that the conviction on obscenity charges of a man who
published a book aimed at children which included highly explicit and
controversial advice on sex was a proportionate and justifiable response
to a threat to morality. The applicant in *Muller*, with his distasteful
paintings, was unsuccessful on the same ground.

In *Otto Preminger Institut v. Austria* (1994) and in *Wingrove v.
United Kingdom* (1996) the Court found no breach where States had
penalised the makers of films which were likely to be seriously
offensive to Christians and recalled that the exercise of freedom of
expression carries with it duties and responsibilities. Amongst them, it
said, in the context of religious beliefs, may legitimately be included a
duty to avoid as far as possible an expression that is, in regard to objects
of veneration, gratuitously offensive to others and profanatory. In
Wingrove, one judge added a separate concurring Opinion in which he
pointed out that the rights of the adherents of other religions would have
received similar protection.

This is not, however, to say that states will always be successful
where the issue relates to a matter other than politics. In *Open Door and
Dublin Well Woman v. Ireland* (1992) the applicants were companies
and individuals who were engaged in counselling pregnant women. An
injunction had been obtained against them to restrain them from
providing information about abortion facilities outside the jurisdiction of
Ireland (where abortion could not lawfully be carried out).

The Court found it appropriate to recall that freedom of expression is
applicable to "information" or "ideas" that offend, shock or disturb the
State or any sector of the population. Such are the demands of that
pluralism, tolerance and broadmindedness without which there is no
"democratic society".

The injunction had been of an absolute nature of the injunction
which imposed a "perpetual" restraint on the provision of information to
pregnant women concerning abortion facilities abroad, regardless of age
or state of health or their reasons for seeking counselling on the
termination of pregnancy. On that ground alone the restriction appeared
to the Court to be over broad and disproportionate.

Moreover, information concerning abortion facilities abroad could be
obtained from other sources in Ireland such as magazines and telephone
directories or by persons with contacts in Great Britain. Accordingly,
information that the injunction sought to restrict was already available
elsewhere.

The Court concluded that the restraint imposed on the applicants from receiving or imparting information was disproportionate to the aims pursued and held that there had been a breach of Article 10.

11. RIGHT TO FREEDOM OF ASSEMBLY (ARTICLE 11)

INTRODUCTION

Article 11 provides:

"1. Everyone has the right to freedom of peaceful assembly and to freedom of association with others, including the right to form and to join trade unions for the protection of his interests.

2. No restrictions shall be placed on the exercise of these rights other than such as are prescribed by law and are necessary in a democratic society in the interests of national security or public safety, for the prevention of disorder or crime, for the protection of health or morals or for the protection of the rights and freedoms of others. This article shall not prevent the imposition of lawful restrictions on the exercise of these rights by members of the armed forces, of the police or of the administration of the State."

This guarantees two rights: freedom of assembly; and freedom of association.

FREEDOM OF ASSEMBLY

Freedom of assembly has not been considered in any great detail by the Court and Commission; but the meaning of the word "assembly" is straightforward enough and some illumination can be gained from the cases, which tend to concern public demonstrations (*e.g. Plattform "Arzte Fur Das Leben" v. Austria* (1991); *Christians against Racism and Facism v. United Kingdom* (1980)). It is clear that the right is applicable both to public and private assembly (*Rassamblement Jurrasien Unité v. Switzerland* (1979)). The right is, however, to *peaceful* assembly and cannot be claimed by those having violent intentions (*G v. Federal Republic of Germany* (1989)).

FREEDOM OF ASSOCIATION

Freedom of association is generally regarded as the right to join with others to achieve a particular end. It includes the right to form and join a political party (*United Communist Party of Turkey v. Turkey* (1998)) and it also includes the right to form and join trade unions. So far as trade unions are concerned, however, the Court has made it clear that Article 11 does not guarantee any particular treatment of trade unions, or their members, by the State, such as the right to be consulted by it (*National Union of Belgian Police Case* (1979–80)). Moreover, in *Young, James and Webster v. United Kingdom* (1981), the Court pointed out that the notion of a freedom implies some measure of freedom of choice as to its exercise. It therefore reasoned that to construe Article 11 as permitting compulsion in the field of trade union membership would strike at the very substance of the freedom it is designed to guarantee (in that case, the applicants had been sacked for refusing to join a union where the industry was subject to a "closed shop" agreement).

INTERFERENCES

Interferences with the rights of freedom of assembly and of association have taken several forms. The mere application of a prior authorisation procedure does not amount on its own to an interference (*Rassamblement Jurrasien Unité v. Switzerland*) but the banning or imposing of conditions upon an assembly or association with lawful intent is very likely to do so. In such a case, the issues will be, as in relation to other Articles, whether the three heads of paragraph 2 are satisfied:

- Is the interference prescribed by law?
- Does the interference pursue one of the specified, legitimate objectives?
- Is the interference necessary (that is, does it address a pressing social need and is it proportionate)?

NECESSITY

As so often, the issues before the Court have related to the question of necessity and, in particular, proportionality. The Court has made a point of saying that it considers each Article 11 case on its own facts and extrapolation from decided cases is therefore difficult and unwise. However, the Commission has held that the banning of trade unions at a Government intelligence establishment was proportionate to the need to maintain national security (*Council of Civil Service Unions v. United Kingdom* (1987)). In *Vogt v. Germany* (1996), on the other hand, the Court held that the dismissal of a state-employed school teacher because she refused to dissociate herself from a left wing political party was excessive. In particular, the Court considered that the concept of the "administration of the state" had to be understood quite narrowly. In *United Communist Party of Turkey* (1998), the Court said that the exceptions set out in paragraph 2 have to be construed particularly strictly where political parties are concerned.

POSITIVE OBLIGATION

There is a clear positive obligation inherent in Article 11. In *Plattform "Arzte Fur Das Leben"* an association of doctors who were campaigning against abortion held two demonstrations which were disrupted by counter-demonstrators despite the presence of a large contingent of police. The applicants complained that they had not had sufficient police protection during the demonstrations and that there had been a violation of Articles 9, 10 and 11 of the Convention. The Court observed that a demonstration may annoy or give offence to persons opposed to the ideas or claims that it is seeking to promote but that the participants must nevertheless be able to hold the demonstration without having to fear that they will be subjected to physical violence by their opponents; such a fear would be liable to deter associations or other groups supporting common ideas or interests from openly expressing their opinions on highly controversial issues affecting the community. In a democracy the right to counter-demonstrate cannot extend to inhibiting the exercise of the right to demonstrate. Genuine, effective freedom of peaceful assembly cannot, therefore, be reduced to a mere duty on the part of the State not to interfere: a purely negative conception would not be compatible with the object and purpose of Article 11. Like Article 8, Article 11 sometimes requires positive measures to be taken.

Having thus established the existence of a positive obligation, the Court considered its content. The Court explained that, while it is the duty of Contracting States to take reasonable and appropriate measures to enable lawful demonstrations to proceed peacefully, they cannot guarantee this absolutely and they have a wide discretion in the choice of the means to be used. In this area the obligation they enter into under Article 11 of the Convention is an obligation as to measures to be taken and not as to results to be achieved. In the instant case, the Court considered that the Austrian authorities did not fail to take reasonable and appropriate measures, so that the positive obligation was satisfied.

---

12. RIGHT TO PEACEFUL ENJOYMENT OF POSSESSIONS (PROTOCOL 1, ARTICLE 1)

INTRODUCTION

Article 1 of Protocol 1 provides:

"Every natural or legal person is entitled to the peaceful enjoyment of his possessions. No one shall be deprived of his possessions except in the public interest and subject to the conditions provided for by law and by the general principles of international law.

The preceding provisions shall not, however, in any way impair the right of a State to enforce such laws as it deems necessary to control the use of property in accordance with the general interest or to secure the payment of taxes or other contributions or penalties."

POSSESSIONS

It will be seen that the Convention uses the word "possessions" primarily, not the word "property". "Possessions" is an autonomous concept, not limited to property rights as recognised by domestic law. It will be understood that "property" is a complex concept even in a single legal system. It is far too complex to form the basis of a rule applicable to over 40 systems.

"Possessions" is wider than most understandings of "property". In *Gasus Dosier und Fördertechnik GmbH v. The Netherlands* (1995) the Court said that it "is certainly not limited to ownership of physical goods: certain other rights and interests constituting assets can also be regarded as 'property rights', and thus as 'possessions', for the purposes of this provision".

So in that case the right was held to apply to the sellers interest in property sold under retention of title, delivered but not paid for and seized by the tax authorities in respect of the purchaser's tax debts. In other cases, it has been held to apply to such disparate "assets" as land occupied for a century but without a formal title (*Matos e Silva v. Portugal* (1996)), a licence to serve alcohol in a restaurant (*Tre Traktorer v. Sweden* (1989)) and certain succession rights (*Inze v. Austria* (1987)).

THE THREE RULES

Introduction

In *Sporrong and Lönroth v. Sweden* (1982) the Court explained the way in which the Article works and the way in which it will be approached by the Court. The Article, the Court said, comprises three distinct rules:
"The first rule, which is of a general nature, enounces the principle of peaceful enjoyment of property; it is set out in the first sentence of the first paragraph. The second rule covers deprivation of possessions and subjects it to certain conditions; it appears in the second sentence of the same paragraph. The third rule recognises that the States are entitled, amongst other things, to control the use of property in accordance with the general interest, by enforcing such laws as they deem necessary for the purpose; it is contained in the second paragraph."

This is not, at first, especially easy to follow; but the Court went on to say that it "must determine, before considering whether the first rule was complied with, whether the last two are applicable". We therefore look first at the second rule, which deals with deals with deprivation of property.

Deprivation of property

For the second rule to apply, there has to have been a taking or expropriation of property. This is not, however, simply a question of whether there has been an expropriation as a matter of law. In *Sporrong and Lönroth* the facts were that the Government had granted the Stockholm City Council a "zonal expropriation permit" covering 164 properties, including that owned by the first applicant. As matters finally stood, the City Council had 23 years within which to expropriate the property. There was an associated prohibition on construction work which subsisted for 25 years. Similar orders affected the second applicant, though for shorter periods of time. The existence of these orders made it exceptionally difficult for the applicants to sell or let their property or to borrow on its security.

The Court noted that the authorities did not proceed to an expropriation of the applicants' properties in the sense that they were not formally deprived of their possessions at any time. This, however, was not the end of the matter. In the absence of a formal expropriation transfer of ownership, the Court considered that it had to look behind the appearances and investigate the realities of the situation. It recalled that the Convention is intended to guarantee rights that are practical and effective and so it had to be ascertained whether that situation amounted to a de facto expropriation, as was argued by the applicants. On the particular facts, the Court held that, although the right in question lost some of its substance, it did not disappear. The effects of the measures involved were not such that they could be assimilated to a deprivation of possessions. There was therefore no room for the application of the second sentence of the first paragraph in the case; but the Court signalled clearly that there could be cases in which something short of legal deprivation of property might amount to deprivation for the purposes of the Convention. That was precisely what happened in *Papamichalopoulos v. Greece* (1993) in which legislation transferred the use of land from the applicants to the Navy Fund, leaving the applicants with a bare and in practice utterly unmarketable title. In that case, the Court held that the second rule applied.

Control of use

In *Sporrong*, the Court, having held that the second rule did not apply, went on to consider the third. That relates to controls on the use of property. The Court held that the prohibitions on construction clearly amounted to a control of the use of the property but that the expropriation permits were not intended to limit or control such use. The third rule therefore applied to the prohibitions on construction.

Air Canada v. United Kingdom (1995), on the other hand, was a case in which there was held to have been a control of use. The facts were that on a number of occasions between 1983 and 1987 incidents of drug smuggling gave rise to concern over the adequacy of the applicant company's security procedures at Heathrow Airport, London. Customs and Excise wrote expressing concern about this and the applicants promised to improve their security. On December 15, 1986 Customs and Excise wrote to all airline operators at Heathrow and Gatwick warning them that consideration would be given to the seizure and forfeiture of aircraft where drug smuggling occurred. On April 26, 1987 a Tristar aircraft owned and operated by the applicants and worth over £60 million, landed at Heathrow where it discharged a container which was found to contain 331 kilograms of cannabis resin valued at about £800,000. The documentation for the container was incomplete and false. On May 1, 1987, at a time when passengers were waiting to board the aircraft, Customs officers seized it as liable to forfeiture. On the same day the Commissioners of Customs and Excise delivered the aircraft back to the applicant company on payment of a penalty of £50,000. The applicants complained to the Commission that the seizure of its aircraft and its subsequent return on conditions violated Article 1 of Protocol No. 1. The Government contended that this was not a case involving a deprivation of property since no transfer of ownership of the applicant's aircraft had taken place. Rather, the seizure and demand for payment were to be seen as part of the system for the control of the use of an aircraft which had been employed for the import of prohibited drugs. The Court held that the Government's analysis was correct and that the seizure of the aircraft amounted to a temporary restriction on its use and did not involve a transfer of ownership. It therefore had to be decided whether the interference with the applicant's property rights was in conformity with the State's right under the second paragraph of Article 1 of Protocol No. 1 "to enforce such laws as it deems necessary to control the use of property in accordance with the general interest". According to the Court, that paragraph had to be construed in the light of the principle laid down in the Article's first sentence, so that it must achieve a "fair balance" between the demands of the general interest of the community and the requirements of the protection of the individual's fundamental rights. There must be a reasonable relationship of proportionality between the means employed and the aim pursued. While the width of the powers of forfeiture conferred on the Commissioners of Customs and Excise was striking, the seizure of the applicant's aircraft and its release subject to payment were undoubtedly exceptional measures which were resorted to in order to bring about an improvement in the company's security procedures. The incident was the latest in a long series of alleged security lapses which had been brought to the applicants' attention. There could be no doubt that the measures taken conformed to the general interest in combating international drug trafficking. Taking into account the large quantity of cannabis that was found and the value of the aircraft that had been seized, the Court did not consider the requirement to pay £50,000 to be disproportionate to the aim pursued, namely the prevention of the importation of prohibited drugs into the United Kingdom.

Peaceful enjoyment of possessions

As regards the prohibitions on construction in *Sporrong*, the question for the Court was whether a fair balance was struck between the demands of the general interest of the community and the requirements of the protection of the individual's fundamental rights. This is proportionality otherwise expressed. In the particular case, the Court held that the applicable legal regime was so inflexible and applied for such a long time as to upset that balance. It therefore found a breach of the Article and did not analyse the matter further; though it had commented, by way of preamble to its judgement, that the expropriation permits affected the very substance of ownership and rendered the applicants' right of property precarious and defeasible. That being so, the Court considered that there was an interference with the applicants' right of property. It seems likely that, had it required to consider the matter, the Court would have found the first rule applicable.

CONDITIONS PROVIDED FOR BY LAW

Whichever of the rules contemplated by the Article applies, an interference with the peaceful enjoyment of possessions must be subject to conditions provided for by law (equivalent to "prescribed by law" in other Articles), in the public interest and proportionate.

PUBLIC INTEREST

The public interest criterion was in the mind of the Court in *Raimondo v. Italy* (1994). In that case, the applicant was prosecuted, and ultimately acquitted, on charges relating to his alleged membership of a mafia-type organisation. In connection with the prosecution, the Italian court had ordered preventive seizure of certain land, buildings and vehicles. It subsequently ordered the confiscation of some of those assets on the ground that it had not been proved that they had been lawfully acquired. Following the applicant's acquittal the return of the confiscated property was ordered. There was, however, delay of over four years in the return of some of the property. The applicant complained that the confiscation had breached Article 1 of Protocol 1 in itself and in that the property had not been adequately supervised and had suffered damage. The Court held that the seizure was:

> "clearly a provisional measure intended to ensure that property which appears to be the fruit of unlawful activities carried out to the detriment of the community can subsequently be confiscated if necessary. The measure as such was therefore justified by the general interest and, in view of the extremely dangerous economic power of an 'organisation' like the Mafia, it cannot be said that taking it at this stage of the proceedings was disproportionate to the aim pursued...the confiscation...pursued an aim that was in the general interest, namely it sought to ensure that the use of the property in question did not procure for the applicant, or the

criminal organisation to which he was suspected of belonging, advantages to the detriment of the community...The Court is fully aware of the difficulties encountered by the Italian State in the fight against the Mafia. As a result of its unlawful activities, in particular drug trafficking, and its international connections, this 'organisation' has an enormous turnover that is subsequently invested, inter alia, in the real property sector. Confiscation, which is designed to block these movements of suspect capital, is an effective and necessary weapon in the combat against this cancer. It therefore appears proportionate to the aim pursued...the preventive effect of confiscation justifies its immediate application notwithstanding any appeal."

As to the damage, the Court held that this was an inevitable consequence of any seizure or confiscation. It was not clear that the damage sustained exceeded that which was inevitable. However, the Court found it hard to see why there had been such a long delay in returning property to the applicant and in that respect (but only in that respect) there was a breach of Article 1 of Protocol 1.

PROPORTIONALITY

Raimondo was, of course, a somewhat extreme case. The Council of Europe has taken a lead in the agreement of treaties to deal with organised crime and its proceeds and a robust approach to any case with that element alleged was to be expected. *Raimondo* should be seen against the background of *AGOSI v. United Kingdom* (1987), in which the Court pointed out that the second paragraph of Article 1 of Protocol 1 recognises the right of a State "to enforce such laws as it deems necessary to control the use of property ... in accordance with the general interest". The Court stressed that there must be proportionality in this and said that the striking of a fair balance depends on many factors and the behaviour of the owner of the property, including the degree of fault or care which he has displayed, is one element of the entirety of circumstances which should be taken into account. The Court also said that there is a substantial margin of appreciation involved in Article 1 of Protocol 1.

13. OTHER RIGHTS

INTRODUCTION

In the foregoing chapters, we have looked at the Convention rights which have generated most case law and which seem most likely to produce significant developments in U.K. law. That cannot really be said about the remaining Convention rights (though they are far from unimportant). They are therefore dealt with in this chapter in rather less detail than the other rights.

ARTICLE 4

Introduction

Article 4 is the prohibition on slavery and forced labour. It provides:

"1. No-one shall be held in slavery or servitude. No one shall be required to perform forced or compulsory labour.

2. For the purpose of this Article the term "forced or compulsory labour" shall not include:

(a) any work required to be done in the ordinary course of detention imposed according to the provisions of Article 5 of this Convention or during conditional release from such detention;

(b) any service of a military character or, in case of conscientious objectors in countries where they are recognised, service exacted instead of compulsory military service;

(c) any service exacted in case of an emergency or calamity threatening the life or well-being of the community;

(d) any work or service which forms part of normal civic obligations."

Slavery

There are two rights here. The first is the right not to be held in slavery or servitude. No case exists in which the Court or Commission have taken the view that a State Party to ECHR was in breach of this and the concept of slavery has not even been considered in any case. "Servitude" was considered briefly in *Van Droogenbroeck v. Belgium* (1982) and found not to be relevant to the case of a convicted prisoner who was required to undertake work in the course of his sentence.

Forced labour

The second right, which is the right not to be required to perform forced or compulsory labour, was considered in *Van der Mussele v. Belgium* (1983). The applicant was a Belgian avocat (lawyer) who had been required, as part of his professional obligations, to act for a person who was indigent and who received no remuneration for so doing. He complained that the fact that he had not been entitled to any remuneration or reimbursement of his expenses gave rise both to "forced or compulsory labour". The case was, in short, one which was not calculated to engage the sympathies of a Court composed of judges who had probably all had to meet similar professional obligations during their careers. However, in the course of holding that there had not been any breach of Article 4, the Court did offer some explanation of the concept of forced and compulsory labour and the case is useful because of that.

The Court said that Article 4 is based, to a large extent, on an earlier treaty of the International Labour Organisation, namely Convention No. 29 concerning Forced or Compulsory Labour. The main aim of that Convention was originally to prevent the exploitation of labour in colonies, which were still numerous at that time and under it, the term "forced or compulsory labour" meant "all work or service which is exacted from any person under the menace of any penalty and for which the said person has not offered himself voluntarily". This definition provides a starting-point for interpretation of Article 4 ECHR but sight should not be lost of the fact that ECHR is a living instrument to be read "in the light of the notions currently prevailing in democratic States".

According to the Court, in the phrase "forced or compulsory" labour the adjective "forced" connotes physical or mental constraint. The second adjective, "compulsory" does not refer to absolutely any form of legal compulsion or obligation. What there has to be is work exacted under the menace of a penalty and also performed against the will of the person concerned, that is work for which he had not offered himself voluntarily. The Court also considered that the work required would have to be disproportionately onerous.

ARTICLE 12

Article 12 simply provides:
> "Men and women of marriageable age have the right to marry and to found a family, according to the national laws governing the exercise of this right."

The Court explained in *Rees v. U.K.* (1986) that the Article is mainly concerned to protect marriage as the basis of the family; and whilst it has been willing to give "family" quite a wide interpretation in Article 8, the Court has not shown itself willing to extend Article 12 beyond marriage as traditionally recognised. This, as the Court pointed out in *Johnston v. Ireland*, reflects the original intention of the Contracting States. The Article also offers some illumination of the concept of the Convention as a "living instrument". In *Cossey v. U.K.* (1990), notwithstanding the significant changes in social attitudes to cohabitation, homosexual and transsexual relation-ships since the entry into force of the Convention, the Court attached some importance to the fact that there was no evidence that there had been any abandonment by Contracting States of the traditional concept of marriage. In that case, and in *Rees* before it, the Court refused to hold that Article 12 entitled a postoperative transsexual to marry in his or her new gender (the terminology becomes difficult—the Court drew distinctions between biological and physical gender and where these are different the appropriateness of words such as "him" or "her" becomes a matter of context and choice of criteria). The reasoning was that the Article gives the right to marry to "men and women" and that it was biologically heterosexual unions that the Contracting States had in mind. The same reasoning would preclude any breach of Article 12 where a State refused to recognise homosexual "marriage" (as the U.K. refuses to do).

The only restriction on the right to found a family recognised by Article 12 is national law. There is a wide margin of appreciation but restrictions must not affect the very essence of the right and must be proportionate; so a Court order which reflected a divorce court's assessment of an applicant's culpability in the break up of his first marriage by prohibiting his remarriage for three years was held to constitute a breach (*F v. Switzerland* (1987)).

PROTOCOL 1, ARTICLE 2

In a study guide, it is gratifying to be able to mention Article 2 of Protocol 1, which provides:
> "No person shall be denied the right to education. In the exercise of any functions which it assumes in relation to education and to teaching, the State shall respect the right of parents to ensure such education and teaching in conformity with their own religious and philosophical convictions."

In practice, the issues have related to the right of parents to insist on particular forms of education and the case law has been concerned chiefly with the limitation of those rights.

It should be noted that the U.K. has made a reservation to this provision, restricting respect for parents' rights to that which is compatible with efficient instruction and the avoidance of unreasonable public expenditure. The effect of that, as a matter of international law, is to modify the Protocol to that extent as it applies to the U.K.

In the case law, it has been held that parents have no right to insist on single sex or selective schools (*W and DM and M and HI v. United Kingdom* (1984)); and that there is no obligation on States to establish or subsidise education of any particular type (*Belgian Linguistic Case (No. 2)* (1979–80)).

PROTOCOL 1, ARTICLE 3

This Article provides:
> "The High Contracting Parties undertake to hold free elections at reasonable intervals by secret ballot, under conditions which will ensure the free expression of the opinion of the people in the choice of the legislature."

In *Gitonas v. Greece* (1986), the Court explained that that the rights thus conferred are not absolute and that States have a wide margin of appreciation in setting conditions for election provided that the conditions set do not curtail the rights to such an extent as to impair their very essence, that they are imposed in pursuit of a legitimate aim and that the means employed are not disproportionate. In that case, a rule that salaried civil servants and others, including members of staff of public law entities, may not stand for election as members of Parliament in any constituency where they have performed their duties for more than three months during the three years preceding the election was held to satisfy these tests.

ARTICLES 16 AND 17 AND THE SIXTH PROTOCOL

We mention these provisions for the sake of completeness. Article 16 provides that nothing in Articles 10, 11 and 14 shall be regarded as preventing the High Contracting Parties from imposing restrictions on the political activity of aliens. It tends to be interpreted rather restrictively and that tendency has been increased by the Treaty on European Union and the rights which it gives to citizens of that Union (*Piermont v. France* (1995)).

Article 17 provides:

> "Nothing in this Convention may be interpreted as implying for any State, group or person any right to engage in any activity or perform any act aimed at the destruction of any of the rights and freedoms set for [in the Convention] or at their limitation to any greater extent than is provided for in the Convention."

On this basis, the Commission dismissed a complaint by applicants who had been prevented from standing for election on a racist platform (*Glimmerveen and Hagenbeek v. The Netherlands* (1979)).

Protocol 6 precludes the death penalty except in limited circumstances in time of war.

ARTICLE 14

Introduction
Article 14 provides:

> "The enjoyment of the rights and freedoms set forth in this Convention shall be secured without any discrimination on any ground such as sex, race, colour, language, religion, political or other opinion, national or social origin, association with a national minority, property, birth or other status."

The treatment of Article 14 in these final pages does not imply that it is residual or an afterthought. It is because Article 14 never stands alone. In terms, it refers to discrimination as to the rights guaranteed by the Convention. It is not a free standing prohibition on discrimination. It always and only operates in conjunction with one of the other Articles. If the discrimination alleged does not relate to a right guaranteed under the Convention, Article 14 does not assist the applicant.

The operation of Article 14

The approach taken by the Court is usually (but not invariably) to begin by considering the substantive Article. If there is a breach of that Article, it does not usually find it necessary to consider Article 14. If, however, there is no breach of the Article, the Court will (if the issue is raised) go on to consider whether there is nevertheless discrimination in the application of the substantive right. Discrimination is a difference in treatment which does not have an objective and reasonable justification.

The way this works appears may be seen from *Abdulaziz, Cabales and Balkandali v. United Kingdom* (1985). In that case, the applicants were women who were lawfully settled in the U.K. In accordance with immigration rules in force at the time (which were a product of the transformation of the British Empire into the Commonwealth), their husbands were refused permission to remain with or join them. The applicants complained that they had been the victims of discrimination, inter alia on the ground of sex, so that there had been violations of Article 8, alone or in conjunction with Article 14. On the Article 8 point, it was clear that there was an interference with the right to respect for family life; the applicants were being deprived of, or threatened with the deprivation of, the society of their husbands. However, States enjoy a wide margin of appreciation as regards respect for family life and Article 8 does not oblige States to respect the choice of a state of residence by couples who are marrying. The applicants must all have known at the time of marrying of the limitations on their husbands' rights to be in the U.K. and there was therefore no breach of Article 8 taken on its own. Nevertheless, it was easier for a man settled in the U.K. to get permission for his wife to join him than for a woman to get such permission for her husband. The advancement of equality of the sexes is a major goal in the Member States of the Council of Europe, so "very weighty reasons would have to be advanced before a difference in treatment on the ground of sex could be regarded as compatible with the Convention. The Government's argument that male immigrants would have a more significant effect on the labour market than female ones was not convincing. Accordingly, although there had been no breach of Article 8 in absolute terms, it was established that the U.K. treated requests for permission for spouses to immigrate differently according to whether the person already settled in the U.K. was male or female. No sufficient justification having been put forward, the Court held that there had been a breach of Article 8 in conjunction with Article 14.

In *Abdulaziz*, the applicants were female. *Burghartz v. Switzerland* (1994) is an example of the application of Article 14 where the person discriminated against was male. The applicants were a married couple who chose on marriage to use the wife's surname, "Burghartz", the husband putting his own surname before it and calling himself "Schnyder Burghartz". The Swiss authorities registered them both as "Schnyder", refusing to recognise any other formula on the basis that in Swiss law only a wife could put her surname before the family name. As a result, a large number of official documents, including the husband's certificate of his doctorate in history, did not include the "Burghartz" element. The Court, having established that Article 8 is relevant to the question of a person's name, proceeded to consider Articles 14 and 8 together. It found that the difference of treatment between husbands and wives complained of lacked an objective and reasonable justification and accordingly contravened Article 14 taken together with Article 8.

What is important about this is that the Court found it necessary, before considering the question of discrimination, to answer the first question applicable to Article 8—was the right relevant to what had happened? Only then did it address the discrimination point and it did so taking Articles 8 and 14 *together*.

Objective and reasonable justification

Finally, on Article 14, we should pay some attention to the matter of objective and reasonable justification. This expression is derived from the *Belgian Linguistic Case (No. 2)*. In *Darby v. Sweden* (1991) the Court elaborated on this, saying that a difference in the treatment of individuals "will only be discriminatory if it has no objective and reasonable justification, that is if it does not pursue a legitimate aim and if there is no "reasonable relationship of proportionality between the means employed and the aim sought to be realised". When one recalls that Article 14 operates in conjunction with the other Convention rights, as to which legitimate aim and proportionality are essential criteria for establishing whether an interference with the right is permissible, it is understandable that the Court should have wished to analyse Article 14 questions in these terms; and they represent for us, at the very end of the book, territory which should be thoroughly familiar.

CONCLUSION

It is not that long ago that judges were saying that they did not see why they should look at the European Convention on Human Rights at all (*e.g. Kaur v. Lord Advocate* (1981)). Now, sections 2, 3 and 6 of the Human Rights Act 1998 combine to bring about a situation in which Convention rights will be a feature of almost every case which comes before the courts or tribunals.

This book has referred already to the Lord Justice General's remark that "it would be wrong... to see the rights under the European Convention as somehow forming a wholly separate stream in our law". His words are reminiscent of the occasion on which Lord Denning famously compared the effect of that other sort of European law—E.C. law—to an incoming tide, gradually but inexorably covering the land and finding its way into the estuaries and up the rivers (*Bulmer v. Bollinger SA* (1974)). One could treat the incoming tide of Convention rights as a matter for regret and think in terms of our native jurisprudence being swamped or drowned. Such a pessimistic assessment would, however, be wrong. Judge David Edward's assessment is better. It was made under reference to E.C. law and on the occasion of the opening of the refurbished Dutch Training and Study Centre for the Judiciary in October 1996; but it holds good for ECHR and national law as well. In law, as in agriculture, he said, if you allow no fresh water to flow into your fields, they will become stagnant and progressively less productive (Edwards, 1997). The incorporation of Convention rights into our law should, on that basis, be regarded as an opportunity to be embraced—not as a development to be feared.

INDEX

93